The Curious Case Of The Firecrotch: This Is Why We Don't Write Our Memoirs While Drunk, Wil

Melissa Snowdon & Dionysia Hill

Published by House of D publications and Lulu.com

ISBN: # 978-1-291-28446-1

Other books by the same author

The Breaking of M by Melissa Snowdon

Detective Kemp's office is up three flights of stairs and around an impressive sculpture of half-empty packing crates that he keeps meaning to clear away from the corridor. It can't have been easy for this red-headed, overdressed stork to have made it all the way up here, not with a walk like that. Christ, he looks like someone kicked a heron in the backs of the knees and then offered it a fish on the other side of the room.

Kemp pushes his chair back against the windowsill and waits for the kid to start talking.

"Are you Detective Kemp?" asks the knock-kneed bastard with the impossibly pretty face.

Kemp wonders if it's worth gratifying such a stupid question with an answer. His name is, last time he checked it *was*, on the door. Admittedly it's on a sheet of paper because he can't really afford a sign just yet but *goddamn it's there*.

"I am he," Kemp says eventually, opening the window. It's raining, but a damp arm is better than sweating to death in this dank hole. "If you're looking for a job you're out of luck, I had to fire the last secretary when she started asking for paychecks. And you know, it was less that I fired her and more that she stormed out and threatened to sue for wages." He checks the boy out again – it's no great hardship – and notes that there isn't any sign of a pizza box either. "Delivering a letter?"

The boy scowls. "I need your help."

"That's excellent, I need your bank account information."

The redhead pouts, which Kemp admits is extremely pretty, but isn't actually helpful and is definitely not paying his rent either on this shabby office or the pitiful apartment above it.

"You don't understand–"

"I understand I don't have deep enough pockets for charity," he says. "Supposing you show me–"

The redhead sighs an affronted sigh and plops a thin wad of bills on the desk. The uppermost one is a hundred, which Kemp guesses means all the others are probably ones. He's pulled that one enough times himself to know; outside the rain reaches a crescendo and someone who has poor impulse control and a noisy car gets into a fight with someone who has an even noisier one.

"Alright," Kemp says, accepting that a hundred dollars and change is better than no dollars and eviction, "what do you need my help with?"

"I think my boyfriend's been kidnapped," says the redhead, shooting a fantasy that Kemp didn't even know was forming squarely in its delicate spine. Well, fuck.

"Right," Kemp says, pocketing the money and peering up at the boy's distressed face. Eighteen, maybe? "And what makes you think that he hasn't ... left town, stopped returning your calls, or ... whatever?"

It's been such a long time since he actually *dated* someone rather than fucking them in a club toilet that he's not sure he can remember the proper protocol. It's all married women and lonely widows in his line of work.

The redhead – Kemp should probably get around to finding out his name for the invoice – makes a face that suggests he's unhappy with the question, and grabs at the back of the guest chair; the backrest comes off in his hands, which distracts him just enough to stop him from saying anything angry.

"Because he wouldn't do that to me," says the boy eventually. "I know what you're going to say and he wouldn't, okay? His apartment is still full of his stuff but he hasn't been back there, and his phone is switched off."

"Listen, Mr–" Kemp says, leaving him dangling to fill the gap as he looks for a cigarette. There aren't any, just a cranky note from himself about how he's going to succeed in giving up since he's so good at giving up on everything else; the handwriting looks drunk.

"Carriere," says the redhead, sitting carefully on the remains of the guest chair. It doesn't collapse, which Kemp thinks is probably only down to the boy weighing about as much as a damp shirt.

"Fuck kind of name is that?"

"It's *French*," says Carriere irritably, pushing back hair that needs no such attention and fiddling with his admittedly perfect upper lip.

"Never would have guessed from the accent," Kemp mutters, sarcastically, "Mr Carriere. Monsieur Carriere. He's been gone how long?"

"A week."

"A week, and you haven't called the police?"

It's not really a question. Carriere doesn't look like the kind of person – not organized enough – to go to a PI in the first week of searches. If he'd called the police he'd be hanging around the station getting on their nerves and being shouted at to go away, probably. He doesn't look old enough or poor enough to have had his naive certainty in due process shaken to that extent. So there has to be some other reason he's come here, first.

Carriere shakes his head slowly and, in something like a parody of a noir novel, he lowers his gaze and fishes a cigarette out.

"Don't smoke in here," Kemp says abruptly, feeling for a moment like he's not being hypocritical at all. "Sorry. Trying to give it up."

The boy lays the cigarette on Kemp's desk, within reach of his fingers, and sighs. "Davey is ... has always been adamant that I should leave the police out of any dealings with him."

"So he's a criminal," Kemp shrugs, trying to ignore the cigarette and succeeding in staring at it like a fat girl at a pastry, even licking his lips. "Okay."

"That's not—"

"He's either a criminal, has a record, or has some connections who aren't above board." Kemp wrenches his gaze from the cancer stick with difficulty and focuses it on Carriere instead: which in terms of 'things he wants and can't really have for the sake of his health' is no improvement. "Not my problem, but if you're honest with me about what he's involved in I stand a better chance of being able to find him. Was there a note? A message?"

"No," Carriere says, looking out of the window behind him.

"So there's a no ransom requirement yet," Kemp says, and he reaches for his notepad.

It's empty, with a sloppy-drunk note on the backboard reading *buy another notepad.*

"Right. So he's been missing a week, you're convinced he hasn't taken an abrupt vacation from the law, and he told you never to call the police. What does this boyfriend of yours do for money?"

Carriere at least has the decency to look away, back into the depressing wilderness of Kemp's office, when he answers, "He imports things."

"Like?"

"All sorts of things. Plants. Children's toys. Jewelry. Clothes."

"Large quantities of drugs."

Carriere's pale and surprisingly freckleless skin lights up beautifully with angry indignation, flaring big pink rockets through his cheeks. "*No.*"

"Riiight." Kemp raises his hands in mock-surrender. "Well, I'm sure customs didn't know about his shipments of teddy bears either and that's why he doesn't want the police to know. Now. Do you remember when you last saw him?"

Carriere considers this, and while he considers it Kemp puts his hands in his pockets because the alternative is stealing the boy's cigarette and smoking it; he's sure the lighter is still in his desk drawer because it was a present and he's been toying with pawning it for two weeks now. Affection is no match for not-being-homeless, and he's not sure how much he misses Dan anymore anyway.

"It was in the park," Carriere says after a while, chewing his lip. Kemp wishes he'd stop. It's not conducive to his brain functioning at full power.

"Which park," Kemp says, unable to keep the impatience out of his voice. If he'd wanted to spend his life trying to wring information out of idiots he'd have become a teacher, not a detective.

Carriere makes a feint with his hand. "You *know*, the one where all the older guys–"

"Ugh," Kemp says before he can stop himself, weary of the game. "Right. That one. What a surprise."

"It was there. We walked. There was some, you know, some making out–"

"Inevitably," Kemp says, "and then what? You went home, he went home, and–?"

"And I was supposed to be seeing him that evening but he never called. I thought perhaps he'd had a change of heart, was tired perhaps – you aren't *uncomfortable* hearing this, are you?" Carriere stops, and stares at him intently for a minute. "I mean, the ... the homosexuality."

Kemp stares back at him with equal intensity, wondering if he should break out the *do I look remotely straight to you* or whether there is no chance of actually penetrating the apparently military-grade stupidity in Carriere's pretty little head.

"No," he says evenly, "I'm actually deeply grossed out by your deviant lifestyle, but I'm also a professional and I like *money*. So we're good."

A woman in the street outside informs everyone in earshot of precisely how wet she is. Carriere narrows his absurdly pretty eyes and says, "Since I can't go anywhere else..."

"Carry on," Kemp says looking down at the cigarette on his desk. Carriere follows his

11

gaze, picks up the cigarette and slots it angrily into his mouth. "I said no smoking."

Carriere scowls and puts the cigarette behind his ear, immediately transformed into some 50s teen idol.

"Skimp on the details regarding *sex*," Kemp advises. His throat constricts at the word and he ignores it; masturbating to memories is a perfectly acceptable alternative to being able to afford cover charges to clubs.

"So I called him but his phone was off," Carriere said, "and then I went to sleep."

Kemp pictures him stamping off to bed for a sulky date with his own hand and then wishes he hadn't; it's a dangerously alluring image.

"And," Kemp prompts.

"And when I called the next day his phone was off too." Carriere sighs. "I went to his apartment the day after and that was - as I described. None of his things are missing. I have a key."

"Right," Kemp repeats.

"I can show you–"

He shakes his head. "Not yet. Tell me what happened first." For all he knows the man's apartment is on the other side of town, and it will be more prudent to meet Carriere there than to have to admit that he's sold his car and needs to walk however many miles it turns out to be.

"His apartment was the way it should have been, and nothing was missing, and nothing had been broken into, I think. But I couldn't find his phone and it was still switched off." Carriere bows his head. "No one has seen him since before I met him in the park. I don't think he even got home that night."

Kemp does not bring up the possibility that Davey is dead, because there is no point, and it doesn't, right now, seem all that likely. Most people who vanish for a week are just being inconsiderate dickheads. So many of his cases have ended that way.

"Okay," he says, instead, "you need to tell me as much as possible about your boyfriend so I can get a good idea of where to start looking. Starting with the rest of his *name*."

"Sickert," says Carriere, which makes Kemp pause with his pen over the backboard. It sounds vaguely familiar, but it's entirely possible that he's imagining it. Or that it's only familiar to Drunk Wil, an entity so separate from Kemp himself that he has his own shelf in the fridge and his own string of horrific exes with whom Kemp would rather have no contact.

"Fantastic. Now, everything *else*?" Kemp prompts, scribbling the name down. It looks familiar written down, too, although his sober handwriting is a good deal more legible than Drunk Wil's.

"I ... I have a picture," Carriere says uncertainly, patting his trouser pocket for a moment. "In my, in–" He extracts his cell and turns the display to Kemp. It's not one of the obnoxious expensive smart-phones, but it's clearly new enough to be capable of taking and displaying pictures like the grainy one being waved in front of him over the desk.

Kemp's own cell phone is held together with duct tape and turns itself off in wet weather which – given the city in which he's ended up – is tantamount to saying that it doesn't work at all.

Davey Sickert looks, Kemp thinks when he's snatched the phone out of Carriere's hand and held it steady enough to actually see the candid taken in what looks like a bathroom, he looks like the kind of person who couldn't impersonate a respectable businessman if he was given a budget the size of the federal deficit. What with the extremely visible tattoos and the sleepy, sneering eyelids as he turns his head toward the camera. Something nags at the back of Kemp's mind, but he's not sure whether it's a hunch, a memory, or the desire to crack open a bottle.

Kemp examines Carriere beyond the phone again. Oh, it's the classic story of naive pretty idiot and disgusting pervert, and the worst part is that this time he isn't the disgusting pervert (or the naive pretty idiot, although that was long ago now); he's tempted to say that the world cannot possibly mourn Sickert and that he'll show up again in a couple of days without anyone doing anything *anyway*, but that would be throwing away free money and the chance to frustrate himself peering at an obnoxiously attractive face for a bit.

"Alright," he says, eventually. "I will take the case. I will invoice you when it comes to a conclusion or you fire me, but you *will* pay me or horrible, horrible things will happen to you."

Carriere looks affronted. "Of course I will pay you."

Fantastic, now he actually has to *work*.

"Alright, I'll take a look at that apartment, first," he says, making a mental note to look up as much as he can on Sickert, assuming the password to the police system that Shaun gave him is still good. "Key?"

"What?" Carriere asks. He surely cannot be this stupid, although in Kemp's estimation he'd have to be as dumb as a whelk to make up for all that beauty.

"Key. I can break into his apartment but that's just going to make matters worse."

"No, I just meant... I can show you–"

Oh great. Now he has to work looking over his shoulder all the time? At that ridiculously pretty face? How's he going to concentrate? Drunk Wil makes an insistent demand in the back of his brain, and Kemp jogs the desk as he gets to his feet.

"Lay on, MacDuff."

"What?"

"Lead. The fucking way."

"Oh," Carriere looks uncertain. "I don't have a car, is that–"

"Neither do I," Kemp says, "so this is going to be a slow journey."

"Yeah but I have a bike," Carriere says, edging his way around the boxes in the corridor with little approaching grace. "Is that okay?"

"Please tell me you don't mean a ... a fucking ... whatever it is you hipster bastards ride. Fixie."

"No," Carriere looks insulted, "I mean a motorbike-bike, you know."

"Oh, good," Kemp says, "then as the investigator on your case, I'm going to have to drive–"

"But I know where his apartment is and you don't."

Fucking logic.

As Kemp found he suspected, the motorbike is little more than a putt-putting push-bike with an engine and he's hardly sure it will take both of them, except Carriere weighs approximately nothing.

He sits awkwardly behind Carriere in the rain, no helmet, his shirt sleeves rolled up and his knees hunched against the boy's alarmingly warm back, and hopes to god that he doesn't get spotted by anyone he knows, riding bitch on the back of a chicken-chaser.

"Okay," Carriere says, over the damp splutter of the little engine, and the bike jerks away.

In theory Kemp ought to lean forward, keep a low profile, bury his face into the boy's jacketless back; in practice he just slouches on the pillion and inhales car exhausts as the rain flattens his hair against his head.

It's not like he can slow the bike down any *more*.

The city slithers past slowly in a damp smear of colors, cars, screeching arguments and the first glimmerings of night light, automatics tricked into pinging on by the low sun that has actually made it through the fat blanket of clouds.

It's a ride too long to Sickert's apartment building. Kemp spots three bars he recognizes and only one of them because he's been thrown out of it. It makes him thirsty, but the little bike just putt-putt-putters on past, barely outstripping the pedestrians on the sidewalk. They could have gone faster on a mobility scooter.

It's a nice part of town. A suspiciously nice part of town in one of the old just-post Confederate buildings that still has the touch of decadence to it; remembering what he saw of the guy in the grainy phone photo, Kemp's not surprised.

What does surprise him is that someone who looks like that can apparently afford to live here, "importing" goods.

"Here," Carriere says unnecessarily, poking an access code into the security gate. 11271. It's not as if he goes out of his way to shield it. Kemp has a brief premonition as to how someone might, say, snatch Sickert from his apartment.

The stairs are mercifully cool and tiled, and he drips on them like laundry as Carriere leads the way; the elevator it seems is not immune to the effects of the grotesquely damp air any more than the one in Kemp's building.

As front doors go Sickert's is relatively unassuming, but all that changes the minute Carriere fumbles his keys out and unlocks the three deadbolts. The interior is ... Kemp hesitates to think *squalid*, because he's appropriated the term for his own living conditions, and besides, this is the kind of squalor only the wealthy can afford. It's *decadent*, which should really come as no surprise.

There are clothes, magazines, cell phones (he counts at least four from where he's standing), jewelry, and fliers everywhere. There are framed prints and there are peeling posters. There are enormous photographs of extremely attractive naked men. There is also – in the middle of the living room, where he'd normally expect a table of some sort – a paddling pool with a chopping board floating in it.

There are empty champagne bottles lurking in every corner and rotting flowers filling up what look like expensive glass vases. He's sort of considering the possibility that Sickert could have merely become lost in his own apartment.

The bedroom is, in the end, what derails his carefully-constructed sense of equilibrium and leaves Kemp leaning on the doorframe, patting his pockets for cigarettes that aren't there.

He's never before encountered the possibility that furniture could have personality, beyond "malicious" (and then only when it barks his shin in the middle of the night; or more accurately, assaults Drunk Wil and reaps the splintering reward). This isn't the case there. There are a lot of things in the room which he can dismiss as mere furniture, but the bed isn't one of them.

The bed exudes sex. He's not even sure how it does it. Maybe there's a pheromone spray under the mattress. It's about the size of an actual apartment and there is a vile mess of sheets in contrasting textures, some sinful-looking pillows, and a lot of empty lube packets. A lot, a lot of empty lube packets. It's really not at all difficult to picture Carriere writhing around on it in naked, sweaty ecstasy with Sickert and a bottle of champagne. It is in fact almost irresistibly easy to picture.

Kemp discovers he's rubbing his lower lip speculatively when Carriere asks if he needs to see the bathroom as well and if he's spotted any clues.

"I've spotted that your boyfriend isn't a real huge believer in 'a place for everything and everything in its place'," Kemp grunts, using sarcasm to cover for what he's sure is an indecently long pause and an unusually flushed face.

Kemp shrugs and tries to shake off the sensation that the bed is leering at him. It would be bad, and probably impossible anyway, to fuck his client on the first day of the case. Apart from anything the boy would probably expect a discount or something.

He acquiesces to the bathroom more in the hopes that the absence of the fucking bed – oh, the fucking bed – will soothe the part of him that thinks it ought to be getting laid more than in the hopes of finding one of those ever-elusive "clues", but to his surprise in the avalanche of hair products, shaving foams, and moisturizers around the basin (he does not risk a glimpse in the palatial bath; last time he looked in one there were bits of someone he knew in it) there's a business card stuck in the rim of the mirror.

Kemp picks the card out with thumb and forefinger and shows it to Carriere.

"I don't know him, he's just someone Davey works with," Carriere says a touch impatiently.

"Just someone Davey works with," Kemp echoes, raising his eyebrows. "Have you ever met Sharpe?"

Carriere shakes his head sullenly, squinting at the card. It occurs to Kemp that it's possible part of the boy's dunderheadedness could be down to the pressing need for glasses. "No. It was his business, not my business. I don't import. I model."

Oh I bet you do, Kemp thinks, somewhat unkindly.

"Well, this guy that your boyfriend just works with has the world's flimsiest cover

23

business and shifts several tons of smack a year." Kemp puts the card in his pocket. "Which would make him a logical person to start with if I had a boner for dying soon."

Carriere scowls and pouts at the same time. "Maybe he doesn't know–"

"Carriere, listen to me. There is not a person on this earth who doesn't know how Sharpe makes his money. The only reason he isn't rotting in jail forever is because he has a very special and incestuous relationship with some very powerful men in most of the important agencies." Kemp brushes his soggy hair back off his forehead and says, "Fortunately for you, I know some people who know some people who work for Sharpe and who won't pull my liver out of my nose if I ask them a couple of polite questions."

Carriere leans on the bathroom doorway, effectively trapping him in the room, which has no windows: only a skylight which Kemp can't reach. "I don't–"

"Yes you do understand."

Carriere shakes his head stubbornly. "There must be some mistake."

"Maybe," Kemp sighs, giving up. "But Sharpe's business card is right there, and I need to pursue it. So if you don't mind getting out of my way–"

With a wounded sigh, Carriere moves out of the way enough to let Kemp out without quite touching him; it's still a close fit, and Kemp has to inhale to keep from brushing any part of his drying clothes on Carriere's still-damp designer rags.

"Detective Kemp," says Carriere, once Kemp's half-way out of the apartment, tripping on vests that probably cost more than his entire outfit, dripping condensed rainwater onto the odd book as he goes.

Kemp doesn't bother to answer, just stands in the hallway with his eyebrows raised and a fat, greased raindrop trekking incongruously down the length of his nose; he'd brush it away, but it would look silly.

"Er. Thank you for agreeing to take the case," Carriere says, awkward and in that moment excessively French. He makes some pointless gesture near his face and Kemp notices the cigarette's still there, flattened and crushed against his copper hair by the motorbike helmet.

"It's not like I had a shittonne going," Kemp admits, leaving.

* * *

The office looks danker and tinier than ever when he returns to it, soaked to the bone and craving a cigarette like he's going to die without one; Kemp stares around the room, exhales a *fuck this*, and after slamming the window shut he stomps upstairs to his distinctly less palatial apartment.

In theory it ought to be a simple case, if a more dangerous one than he'd like. Find one of his contacts, get them to see if there have been any Sickert-shaped body disposals recently, and if not, assume he's AWOL for a while and sit around and wait for the decadent bastard to come back and start tupping his piece again.

And it shouldn't be complicated by the presence of a bone-dumb extraordinarily pretty alleged model with knees like an outraged wading bird, but it's been a very long time since Kemp remembers having sober sex with anyone.

He can't really account for what Drunk Wil has and hasn't done, of course, but then Drunk Wil isn't really *him*. He's just in control of the same body, when Kemp's reached the appropriate levels of inebriation.

Kemp walks over the top of a pile of clothes and some empty pizza boxes and realizes only when he reaches his bed that he's also walked over the low table that came with the place too. But it's irrelevant, the idea has already taken root. *Drunk Wil* can deal with the nagging desire in his lower belly, *Drunk Wil* can masturbate himself sore over the thought of Carriere and Sickert locked in a sticky deviant embrace in that whore of a bed, and Kemp can maintain professionalism with his client.

It takes far too long to marshal his resources. The fifth of vodka he thought he had turns out to be an empty bottle. There are two half-empty whiskey bottles under his bed and a third mostly-full one which Drunk Wil appears to have stashed down the back of the

TV for reasons that Drunk Wil has chosen not to share with him.

The combination of these bottles gives him enough to abandon responsibility, at least; Kemp falls on his back on his bed, and crushes god knows what under him as he does so (there's definitely a shoe in there, and that's going to smart), and cracks open one of the more empty bottles.

Carriere has a mouth designed for sucking cock. That much is very clear.

(*Nope, still too sober*)

Kemp undoes his pants and finishes the rest of the bottle in an expansive swallow. Once upon a time when he was naive and pretty and a moron like Carriere, guys used to go wild over watching his throat work like that. Now they just throw him out of bars.

Carriere's got a neck he could sink his teeth into and leave vicious brown-red bruises in the snow-white skin, like stab marks on cotton.

(*No, still too sober and a little scared of himself*)

He cracks open another of the half-finished bottles and necks it as quickly as he can. Carriere has collarbones that Kemp could probably shave himself with. Going by the state of his lips, his nipples are probably pink as candy. Kemp tugs lazily on his own pubes as the room begins to swirl and shimmer. Carriere would probably make some high, throaty noise every time Kemp thudded home into his ass.

* * *

When Kemp wakes the next morning he's still mostly-dressed and hugging a nearly-empty bottle of whiskey that he recognizes as the full bottle from behind the TV the night before; his pillow is balled up under his crotch, and when he pulls it out it's as he feared - crusted with come and ripped on the casing seams.

"Fuck, Drunk Wil," Kemp mutters, throwing it in the direction of his laundry bag. "You animal."

But he resigns himself to his lowly station for the time being: no matter how inadequate the shower, it will help with the hangover and there's no way he can pursue even the most cursory of investigations with – Kemp looks down at his now bare legs and sighs – with dried semen stinking up his graying pubes.

The shower spits a pathetic dribble of lukewarm water over his face and chest, and he can't help thinking *I came more than this last night*, just based on the evidence of how much of his bedding he's going to need to either launder or *incinerate*. Still, there aren't many apartments whose landlords will take rent in blowjobs and forged Target gift cards. He has to make do.

The hot water – well, the water which isn't entirely freezing – runs out before he's even managed to work up a lather with his cheap, virulent orange soap in his pubes, and Kemp considers revising his opinion of "making do". He also considers scrubbing himself with the remains of the whiskey, but he knows he smells bad enough already.

Kemp is shivering even in the oppressive summer heat by the time he's finished scraping the remnants of Drunk Wil's excesses from his body. He's still not sure he can face food yet, though.

Instead of facing up to the total absence of nutritious, non-cockroach food in his apartment, Kemp wraps a dirty t-shirt around his head as a towel and climbs down the box-strewn stairs from his garret to his offices, naked from the waist up. After all, it's not as if anyone's going to come and bother him at – Kemp checks the wall clock and sighs – 88:88am.

He stabs the number into his phone without hesitation, but hovers his finger over the call button. Is it really worth getting into anything with one of Sharpe's boys to find some temporarily mislaid deadbeat who probably flosses his teeth with boys like Carriere anyway?

Kemp sighs. The *entire billfold* had been hundreds. If he doesn't at least try he's going to have to hand that back.

He hits *call*.

Farinaux picks up on the second ring, and from the sound of his voice Kemp dragged him out of bed. He realizes he has absolutely no idea of the time beyond "the sun is vaguely shining and I feel like I'm going to die of sweat", which puts him anywhere between 8am and sunset.

"Wilberforce," Farinaux says. Kemp doesn't correct him, but he's a little disturbed that Farinaux apparently thinks he starts drinking the minute he wakes up.

"Leo," Kemp says, leaning back in his divinely uncomfortable chair, the nasty fabric sticking to his bare back. He rubs the rough location of his back tattoo as if it's still itchy and healing, because Farinaux has that effect on him. The tattoo isn't something he's proud of – it showed up after almost a whole week of Drunk Wil's adventures and scared him off drinking for nearly a whole weekend – but it does seem to have placed him in the good graces of some people he ordinarily wouldn't have stood a chance of charming. He darkly suspects that it *means something*. "I need a favor."

"You always do," Farinaux sniggers, sounding bored and interested. "It will cost you."

"It always does," Kemp says, rolling his eyes to himself as he goes through the ritual of looking for cigarettes that aren't there. He stops just before he pats his chest for cigarettes in the breast pocket, which, given that he's wearing only sweat and craving, would be especially stupid.

"So you're flush, then?" Farinaux yawns. "Not paying in blowjobs this time? Not that I mind..."

Kemp winces and taps his finger on the desk. *Drunk Wil, goddamnit, you asshole.*

"I'm good for the bills this time, Leo," Kemp says, resisting the urge to thump his forehead off the desk in time with his finger. "Can we meet? I need to ask you a couple of things about someone you might know."

"I'm not ... busy," Farinaux says, and Kemp can hear the raised eyebrows in his voice. "But you don't wanna be seen around my part of town, not right now. Sharpe might want to duck your face in a toilet, if you follow me?"

"That was brilliantly clear, thank you, Leo."

"So why don't you crawl around to Philippe's bar and–"

"Because I'm banned."

"–Adrian's–"

"Also banned."

"What the fuck have you been up to, Wil?"

Kemp rubs his face, scratches abruptly under his t-shirt turban, and says in a low voice, "Now if I remembered that it wouldn't be any fun, would it?"

Farinaux snorts. "Alright. Fucking Starbucks. You haven't been banned from Starbucks."

"Which one?" Kemp scratches under his t-shirt again, and his stomach gives a cautious rumble. He's going to have to head out anyhow, head out or feel worse pretty soon.

"Main Square, opposite Lane Bryant," Farinaux says, smirking all through his voice. "You can buy me a latte or a fuckoccino or whatever and ask me your questions."

"You're right, I'm not banned from that one," Kemp agrees. "Give me five mi–"

Kemp twitches in his seat and nearly falls out of the chair.

"–I'll get back to you."

He drops his phone on the desk and stares at Carriere, standing in his doorway with his head to one side and his hands in his shockingly tight pockets. Kemp removes his t-shirt from his head slowly, and pulls it, wet and soapy, down onto his chest.

"Have you–?" Carriere begins, but Kemp cuts him off with an impatient slap on the desk.

"Would you mind not nagging me like someone's wife when I'm trying to pursue your fucking case, Carriere?"

"... Claude," Carriere says, looking as if Kemp's just walked over and slapped his pretty face: complete with burning pink spots on his cheeks which Kemp has to admit, even in his irritation, is arrestingly attractive.

"What?"

"My name is Claude."

"Right, well, you're my client, so you're Mr. Carriere, and I can't find your fucking boyfriend with you leaning over my shoulder every five minutes. I have to go and talk to a very ill-connected man, and you're not coming with me."

"I was just checking to see if you needed any more information," Carriere says, sulkily. He lurks in the doorway for a second, "Or a ride to Main Square."

Kemp deflates slowly. "How professional I will look, turning up on the back of your child's toy of a motorbike, Carriere," he says, getting up. He looks down at his bare feet and mutters, "Let me get some shoes if I have to ride bitch to see my contact."

"Sure," Carriere says, sounding exceptionally French. His eyes follow Kemp across the room, strafing his body with pale red eyelashes, and he does that same thing he did back in Sickert's apartment, sticking in the doorway as Kemp slips past him.

Kemp stands on something small and sharp on his way back up stairs, and limps, tracking spots of blood on the bare floorboards with a sense of gratitude that the discomfort takes his mind off his recent proximity to Carriere.

He needs to get himself together; more than that, he needs to get himself laid so that he doesn't keep going demented over pretty clients. Get *himself* laid, and not Drunk Wil.

Kemp swears his way through the apartment and throws his shoes on without washing or even wiping the blood from his sole.

When he returns Carriere has stopped lurking in the door to his office and is instead occupying the head of the stairs down to the lobby, which at least means he doesn't have to slither past him on tip-toes again.

"Right," Kemp says, feeling oddly jangled just being in the boy's presence - it smells like he's wearing some sort of cologne today and he's not sure if it's an improvement. "But you can't come into Starbucks because it will fuck this whole thing up, he can't see you. It could potentially put you in danger."

Carriere stares at him incredulously all the way down the stairs but doesn't actually say anything until he's handing over a spare helmet to Kemp, and then all he says is, "Really put me in danger?"

"You remember what I said about Sharpe?"

Carriere swallows, and Kemp swears internally as the image of what *else* he could be persuaded to swallow springs to mind and, shortly after, to groin.

He's making it up, of course. Farinaux doesn't give a shit about some mindless pretty-boy hanging around except that he'll demand a go on Carriere in exchange for information if he realizes Carriere's his client. Kemp slides into bitch position on the bike and leaves the chinstrap hanging. It's easier to keep Carriere in the dark than deal with Farinaux's sleazy demands.

"Hang on," Carriere says. It's the last thing he says to him for a good twenty minutes – the traffic is not great – but Kemp gets a nose full of his cologne every time the bike stops and his face is pitched into Carriere's back. It doesn't exactly encourage him to maintain a good seat.

He leans forward to clutch at Carriere's shirt-back as a cop drones past on a slightly quicker-moving motorcycle, and ducks his head in spite of the helmet, trying to hide the loose straps.

"You're the worst passenger ever," Carriere says, when he dismounts. "Do you know how many times I could have crashed because of you throwing your weight around?"

Kemp thinks that *throwing his weight around* is something he's hardly had much practice in, but instead he hands the helmet back to Carriere and says huffily, "That's because I'm one of nature's drivers."

"Not on my bike."

"Listen, I have to go and talk to this guy *alone*, okay? I – go and do something somewhere else."

Kemp waves a dismissive hand at the pretty boy, and inwardly savors the moment. It's been a long time since he's been able to tell someone that outwardly wholesome to fuck off.

He alters his walk almost subconsciously as he heads for the Main Square Starbucks, changing it from his usual stiff stumble to a more louche saunter, and by the time he gets to the front door he wonders if he's overdoing it from the looks he's getting.

Farinaux is draped over one of the comfy chairs like exceptionally dirty laundry. The sound system is playing some ill-advised Bob Dylan Starbucks-only release that makes Kemp wish he didn't have ears (Bob Dylan's voice is an affront to human dignity as far as he's concerned). As the door closes behind Kemp, the skies split like a punched face and drool fat globs of rain down the windowpanes with an accompanying sub-bass mutter of thunder.

Kemp feels this is possibly a bad omen, but if he went around paying attention to omens he'd never get out of bed.

"Wil," Farinaux says, waving indolently from the rust-colored cushions. "I tried to get you your usual but they don't sell large bottles of cheap liquor in here, even when you ask nice."

"Leo," Kemp says, sliding into the seat opposite and automatically putting his feet on the table. "You're not funny."

"TAKE YOUR FEET OFF THE TABLE, SIR," calls one of the baristas in the tone of voice that says she's yelled this at him before, most likely at Drunk Wil, and had a lengthy and descriptive hail of abuse in return.

This time he whips his feet off the table top and pretends that he was going to do it anyway.

"Oh, but you want a favor, Wilberforce, so I am hilarious," Farinaux says, picking a raspberry out of his muffin and chewing it lazily. He keeps his hand near his mouth, which would be an excellent flirtation tactic if Kemp didn't hate him and harbor a suspicion that Farinaux is the one responsible for a former and expensive trip to the doctor for some antibiotics.

And alright, Farinaux is attractive in the way that Sickert is – tattooed, louche, arrogant – and he probably doesn't smell as bad as Kemp probably does (fortunately the smell of coffee and the memory of Carriere's infuriatingly nice cologne is masking any evidence), but Kemp has this preference for not being flirted at by people who he'd kind of rather see arrested and possibly eaten alive by angry weasels.

Farinaux isn't exactly in the upper echelons of the drugs pyramid, but he's not the end user and he's not one of the desperate kids and pregnant chicks doing the nasty, risky, low-status stuff for them either, and Kemp has it on the authority of his own (now-deceased) miniature camera that

41

violence toward people who do not deserve it has been in his repertoire more than once.

"You know Sickert?" Kemp asks, trying to force a smirk onto his face as he leans forward, rather than folding his arms across his chest and giving Farinaux the cold gimlet stare he deserves.

"Who doesn't," Farinaux says with exactly the kind of leer that Kemp knows to interpret as *know, Biblically*. "What do you want on him?"

"He works for or with Sharpe, right?"

Farinaux rolls his eyes. "Oh WilbyWil. What rock have you been living under? He's Arm A2 of getting things into the country. Fluffy teddy bears and DVD-Rs and Dolls of America all stuffed full of smack."

Kemp only shrugs. "Figures. They haven't fallen out at all? No money owed?"

"Do you want some of my muffin?" Farinaux says, tipping the plate toward him. "It's nice. Look. It's got fruit in it. You could eat that and maybe you won't die of HIV or whatever it is that makes you such a boner-killer when you're sober."

"And a healthy helping of barista-sweat, no thanks." Kemp holds up a hand. "You're sure there's no bad blood, no reason for Sharpe to have him vanished?"

"Nope," Farinaux says, inserting about half a muffin into his mouth at once. "They're like–" he crosses his fingers and holds them up. "Good buddies. Business is booming, everyone is happy. Why?"

"Because he's missing."

Farinaux scrubs crumbs off his teeth with the end of his finger while the rain plays a sullen tattoo on the window. "First I've heard."

"He's been gone a little over a week..." Kemp says, wondering if he eats as messily as Farinaux. There's been no one to actually test his culinary skills up against and while Mama didn't raise no slob, he's aware that Mama also didn't raise him to get blind drunk for five day periods, fuck strangers in public bathrooms, or live in an apartment so gross that the cockroaches were petitioning to leave, either.

"Sure he's not just holed up in his love nest fucking that retarded boyfriend of his?"

Farinaux asks, picking the remains of a raspberry from his molar and examining it before reinserting it into his mouth. "You know who I mean, right? He looks like a girl and speaks English like it was beaten into him in the Soviet Union?"

"France," Kemp corrects. "He's French."

"Who, Cristobel or whatever her name is?" Farinaux says, cocking his head to one side in order to scratch the stubble under his chin. "Nope, from what I can make out he's from one of those buttfuck little post-Soviet states where they eat endless sausages. Practiced in the art of–" he breaks off to mime a blowjob. "You're thinking of the other one, then, the little foxy redhead who walks like he's still got a dick in him."

"I've been to his apartment," Kemp says, filing the information away for future use. For all he knows, Carriere is aware of the arrangement. For all *he* knows, Carriere and this effeminate Eastern European fuckbuddy curl up with Sickert together, which is not a thought process he needs to examine for too long if he's planning on thinking with his *head* at all today.

"Oh he's not going to like that–"

"Then he can try not going missing, can't he."

"Whatever," Farinaux says. "I haven't heard anything about him falling under a tram or shit, but I'll let you know if Sickert shows up – with or without a pulse, okay?"

"Okay," Kemp agrees. "So what do I owe you for this unhelpful help?"

Farinaux leans forward to dump his muffin plate and explosion of crumbs on the table, and in an affected (and appalling) British accent, says, "Give us a kiss, darlin'."

"Hundred bucks?" Kemp asks, reaching into his pocket for the billfold.

"Pfft, please. I wipe my ass with more money than that," Farinaux says with a predatory smirk. "Kisses or I up the ante and we make use of the customer bathroom right the fuck now."

"How come you never became a pimp, Leo?"

"Enough questions from you, Wil," Farinaux says, reaching over the table with his finger crooked. "Pucker up, bitch."

Kemp sighs and says, "All I'm saying is you'd make a killer pimp. That information wasn't worth anything and you're still demanding saliva with menaces."

"And you'd make a sweet-ass whore," Farinaux says, half-rising until his face is almost level with Kemp's, his knees knocking the table. Half the people in this place must be staring by now, but Kemp doesn't risk a sideways look. "Y'know. *Again.*"

With this Farinaux seizes Kemp by the collar and gives him a lengthy and unequivocally sexual kiss; there's no way to pass this off as a friendly and continental peck and it's going to result in some significant hostility from the other customers if he's any judge. Hand-holding they might tolerate, full-on face-sucking is almost certainly out of their comfort zones.

Kemp suspects Drunk Wil is already aware of how good a kisser Farinaux is, but this is his first experience as Sober Kemp, and it's been a long time since anyone kissed Sober Kemp at all. He remembers to keep his hands firmly and rigidly by his sides and to kiss back as little as possible, but it's ha–it's difficult.

Farinaux gets his hand under Kemp's chin the way Kemp used to get his hand under boys' chins back when he actually got to kiss them and remember it. Farinaux has soft lips and a forceful tongue and he tastes of muffin and testosterone and Kemp wants to fuck him.

The thought's in his head before he can stop it, but he holds his legs as rigid as his arms and keeps his tongue as limp in his mouth as he can.

His balls are taking notice. His stomach sends excited love notes up to his heart and tries to commandeer his head: *Hey guys we're onto something here. You could hold him down and fuck his mouth. Come on his face. C'mon.*

He beats down his libido with reason: there is no way on God's or anyone else's earth that Farinaux would let him do that. If anything, he'd be the one on his knees, squinting up at that pervert's smirk through a sheen of semen and sticky eyelashes … and also someone is shouting at them.

"YOU WANT TO MAYBE TAKE THAT SOMEWHERE ELSE?" an irate, fat

man is squawking from his window seat. "THERE ARE CHILDREN HERE."

It takes Kemp, his face still clenched between Farinaux's hands, a little while to spot what kids the guy is talking about - a baby currently grizzling, probably more at the noise than at anyone mashing lips, but the barista's in on the act too, now.

"This is a coffee shop, not a bathhouse," she says, leaning over the till. "Either quit that or get out."

Farinaux releases Kemp and swaggers – there is really no other word for it – over to the fat man by the window. "You want to suck my dick?"

"Christ," Kemp mutters, getting out of his seat as quickly and as quietly as he can. He leaves a twenty on the table on general principles and slinks toward the door, keeping as low a profile as someone his height can.

"No I think you *do* want to suck my dick," Farinaux says loudly, and Kemp can't help cringing. He has this awful feeling, this sense of familiarity that won't leave; this is a move that Farinaux's picked up from Drunk Wil. Jesus. Why isn't the door closer. At least

Farinaux is copping all the attention in the place.

"TAKE YOUR PENIS OUT OF MY FACE."

"My dick isn't in your face but it can be just as soon as you open your mouth properly and stop bleating, you fat, self-satisfied phobe."

Kemp cringes again and slips out into the rain as quietly as he can; it's a matter of brisk walking and keeping his head between his hunched-up shoulders, and then he's back where he left Carriere. Like some sort of unbearably elegant pedigree dog the boy is still there, standing under an awning and smoking a cigarette that Kemp wants so badly he could just about snatch it from Carriere's insanely beautiful lips.

"Was he helpful?" Carriere asks anxiously, his hands in his pockets and a motorbike helmet hanging from each of his delicate wrists.

"No he fucking was not," Kemp says before he can stop himself. "He was his usual fuck-pig self. I need a drink."

"I don't suppose that's going to help your investigation," Carriere says, as if his boyfriend doesn't spent his entire life guzzling Krug and cocaine like it's the elixir of youth.

"It will help my *temper*," Kemp mutters.

"Where do you intend to go next?" Carriere asks, proffering a motorcycle helmet which Kemp has to restrain himself from swatting away.

"Carriere, do you actually understand how an investigation works?"

Carriere glares at him as the rain starts up again, a little more anemic than before. "I am only trying to help you, Mr. Kemp, when you have no car and a lot of places to visit."

"That's an excellent way to get yourself shot," Kemp groans. He's only exaggerating a little. Okay, it's probable that anyone with a connection with Sickert will know Carriere is his property and will steer clear of offending him by murdering his fucktoy. But that only holds *if* the prince of douches is still in the good graces of the major players in the city.

If he's pissed someone off and been put underground they'll want to dispose of anyone connected to him as well. Kemp's been dodging bullets and bad luck in this town for long enough to know that the gangs here favor a "burned bridges and ground sown with salt" approach to retribution.

"Oh you are being very silly," Carriere says almost airily, but there's an uneasiness in his voice that says he may not have been entirely blind to his situation with Sickert. Nevertheless, Kemp is moved to mutter:

"Were you *dropped on your head* as a baby or something?"

Carriere presents him with a perfectly Gallic shrug and holds out the motorcycle helmet awkwardly. "Please, I want to make this as easy as possible for you to find my boyfriend, do you understand?"

"I understand," Kemp says, narrowly avoiding saying *I'm not the idiot here* out loud. He takes the helmet from Carriere and eyeballs him for a minute. "However, in the interests of me being paid for finding Sickert, instead of having to identify your body to the police and answer several awkward questions about *why* you have a double tap to the back of the head–"

"Who says *I* will be the one shot?"

"I *also* don't want to die," Kemp says pointedly. "Okay, I appreciate you're keen for me to find him. I get that you want to help. But you are only slightly more obvious than a black eye and half the people I want to talk to may already have seen you with him."

Carriere snatches the helmet back out of his fingers and snaps, "But you *will* contact me as soon as anything happens?"

"I will give you *daily fucking reports* if it keeps you happy," Kemp growls.

"It will make me happy with my wallet," Carriere says, with a pointed stare. "I can pay you *more* the more cooperative you are."

"Sadly I am a private detective and not a prostitute," Kemp snaps. He keeps the *anymore* part of the sentence firmly inside his own mind, where it immediately nags at him. "You're paying for my ability to milk contacts, not my charming personality."

He waits for Carriere to say *good, because **that** isn't worth a dime*, but Carriere merely sags and trots away to his silly little anemic motorcycle without another word.

Kemp leans against the shop wall behind him for a moment and catches his thoughts wandering around in aimless confusion, having been all geared up for a dirty-fighting shitty argument, only to find themselves robbed of anyone to villainize. He scoops out his phone and reaches for cigarettes that aren't there at the same time. Time to start pestering again.

"Baron," Kemp says when the call connects. He's not sure why Henry Baron floated into his head right now – maybe it was the mention of prostitutes – but he's a convenient enough starting point. "How's it going?"

Around him, a couple of blue-fronted birds of some kind shelter from the rain as it picks up, hopping nervously in the region of his feet.

"Orright Wil?" Baron says, contriving to sound like he is right this minute now having something very pleasant done to his lower half. Kemp munches violently on the inside of his cheek and tries not to picture what could possibly have done that to his tone of voice, rather unsuccessfully. "How can I help youuuu?"

"You could start by not drawling like that," Kemp mutters. "But since you ask, I'm looking for someone."

"Uh-hh-uh," Baron agrees, "you're always looking for someone and it's never me."

"That's because you have diseases."

"Shh," Baron says, hastily, "I have a client, don't say shit like that."

"Stop having diseases then," Kemp says, watching the little birds bounce up to his boots and away again as if they're playing chicken. "Listen, do you have – you know Sickert, right? Davey Sickert?"

"Don't like him, doesn't pay," Baron says very abruptly. "Ohhh, *that's right*."

"Jesus fucking Christ," Kemp mutters under his breath. His face is hot. He's probably going red as a slapped buttock.

"Well I have to make them feel wanted," Baron says in a slightly less pornographic voice. "S'up, Wilberforce? He owe someone money? Wouldn't surprise me."

"As far as I know, he's gone walkies," Kemp says, adopting a phrase he's heard Baron use a number of times, usually in reference to his own – well, Drunk Wil's – abrupt departure from a, from an assignation. "And I was wondering whether you'd seen him, or if anyone else you knew had."

"I don't do Sickert," Baron says huffily, a petulance somewhat undermined by his breathy gasp at the end of the sentence. "You want the numbers of the guys who do?"

"Of course," Kemp says. He's attracting glances from the few people out walking in the rain, but that's normal; once upon a time everyone used to stare at him when he was walking around. It might have been the clothes, of course.

He rummages in his pocket for a pen, can't find one, and is ready to ask Baron to text them to him when Baron replies through what sounds like a bitten lip:

"Then you have to talk to Zeke, don't you."

"Oh thanks, Hank, you're a fountain of generosity," Kemp grumbles. He already has Dempsey's number. He was hoping not to have to use it.

"Hey, I'm talking to you while I'm wor-*ooh*-working. Don't knock it."

Kemp hangs up on him and glares at his phone menu in disgust. There is the small comfort that if he talks to Dempsey, *he* won't be in the middle of having his salad tossed. The downside is that he will be talking to someone who has killed a man with his bare hand and his bare 15 inch neon purple double-ended dildo, which is a matter of public record rather than urban legend.

Dempsey got off, of course, because this town is as corrupt as Sicily and Dempsey knows a lot of well-connected people who don't want their names involved in legal proceedings, but everyone knows it was him. Kemp knows because he was there when it happened, trying and failing to keep his eyes shut and his painfully tight trousers from cutting off circulation to his balls.

It's still raining. Farinaux has probably finished face-raping that fat guy by now, or has left before someone calls the cops, but Kemp is in no mood to risk a public embarrassment by going back into Starbucks. He levers himself off the wall and darts across the street through stationary traffic, shoulders hunched against the half-hearted downpour.

The little coffee shop across the street is usually full of hipsters, which is just one reason among many that Kemp avoids it – he dislikes being mistaken for fashionable when in reality he is merely *poor* – but today there is only a cat asleep on the table and a girl with a black eye and a clump of hair petting at it miserably.

He avoids her gaze, orders a coffee, and slinks away into the far corner with his phone ready again.

He hits dial with a cup of pissy-looking probably-organic-Fair Trade-monks-touched-this coffee at his elbow, and leans his face against the rough brick wall as the phone rings and rings.

When Dempsey picks up, Kemp almost hits the disconnect button in a panic. He clutches at the handle of his stupid hand-made coffee cup instead, and scrapes un-glazed ceramic on his fingers. Fantastic.

"Oh hello," Dempsey says, sounding nothing like as surprised as he ought to – Kemp guesses that fucking diseased prick

Baron must have called ahead of him almost immediately, "Goodness, it's a Wilberforce. Haven't heard from *you* in a long time."

His mongrel accent and soft, dark voice slide around Kemp like a crushing embrace from a disliked relative (Kemp has plenty of those to choose from, a flotilla of be-hatted church-going aunts with perfume not quite blotting out the scent of the liquor and the internal rot), squeezing his chest and stomach together and purring in his ear.

"I need to ask you a couple of things," Kemp says, his tongue unexpectedly dry.

"I gather from Henry that they're not questions like *can I come back and work for you again*," Dempsey says, sounding somewhere between amused and exaggeratedly hurt. The latter gives Kemp the spine-crawling creeps, since the guy always used to make like he was personally wounded before he tore a strip out of someone...

"I just need to talk to a few of your boys about someone they may have seen—"

"Talk my boys about their clients, Wilby? I don't recall that being allowed when you worked for me, do you?"

Kemp suppresses a shiver and reminds himself that he's in a coffee shop outside Main Square, not in a dingy warehouse office some miles outside of town in pants that could seriously damage his chances of ever becoming a father, and he's got a shirt on now and everything. "No, I remember that quite well. I'm just looking for Sickert–"

"Oh *are you?*" Demsey's voice morphs from amused, teasing disinterest into something so sharp that it nails Kemp's gaze to his coffee.

He looks around the coffee shop; there's a ticking clock in the shape of an owl. The counter has vegan fucking "chocolate" brownies stacked up high. There's no sign of the barista, who is in all probability out back smoking a joint, and the girl with the black eye is crying into the fur of the tolerant cat as silently as she can.

No one is lurking here to shove something silicone so far down his esophagus that his stomach lining ruptures, leaving him to simultaneously asphyxiate and die of stomach acid eating through his flesh.

"He's missing," Kemp says, putting his thumb knuckle in his mouth.

"Well when you *find* him, you make sure to ask about the two thousand he owes me," Dempsey says. He makes it very clear that "ask" should involve some sort of blunt instrument. Kemp gnaws on his knuckle, and somewhere inside him Drunk Wil peevishly demands a drink.

"I would have thought that was pocket change to someone like–"

"Then he can reach into his fucking pockets and *pay me*," Dempsey hisses. Kemp jerks the phone away from his ear and bites hard enough on his knuckle to draw blood.

"So can I talk to–" he says, when he's stopped bleeding into his own mouth. Kemp dislikes the way his voice is going grey around the edges, almost as if it's copying his hair.

"No, I'll talk to them. They're not supposed to be dealing with that prick until he pays up, but some of them are moody little bitches," Dempsey says. Kemp draws a line between *moody little bitches* and the results of their back-talking, and sighs to himself. He is dripping blood from his hand onto the table and if the barista isn't *totally* stoned when he gets back he's going to be pissed. "I'll call you back."

Kemp considers saying *there's really no need for that*, but he is unfortunately still conducting an investigation here. He thinks of Carriere's disturbingly pretty pout, measuring that and a stack of hundreds against the remembered sound of a man dying with a throat full of fake cock in a bleak warehouse. Fuck.

Dempsey ends the call and for the rest of the coffee cup, Kemp ignores the twitching in his thigh and the ominous feeling in his stomach, and slightly more successfully also turns his attention away from the now-sleeping cat and the girl blowing her nose on the other side of the coffee shop.

It's stopped raining outside; he leaves a dollar on the table and slips out past the girl as she takes out her phone from her bag. He guesses she hasn't been mugged, then.

It's not that he's out of contacts to chase, but Kemp heads for home; his legs demand it before his brain gets a word in edgeways – it's still taken up with Not Remembering and accidentally remembering. And Drunk Wil is clamoring to be let out, and it's – well, it's probably afternoon by now, and there has been enough work for one day, enough brushing his already tarnished halo up against the filth of the city all over again.

It takes more than an hour to trudge back to his building, and by the time he gets back there he's drenched through to some internal organ or other. Along the way he's considered possibly calling Carriere and demanding a ride, but he's not sure that being wet and traumatized on the back of a shitty bike behind a pretty idiot is any better than his current situation, and given how long it's been since he got laid *that he can remember*, it might actually be worse.

He finds himself outside a liquor store before he finds himself outside his building; there's a gap in his memory which disturbs him more than he cares to admit: Drunk Wil is only supposed to be in charge *when he is drunk*. That's sort of the point.

However, he's missing a hundred bucks and he has some very heavy paper sacks in his arms, along with the distinct feeling that someone has just asked him if he's planning on a party.

Kemp shakes off the feeling that someone is walking over his grave and trots as quickly as he can back up to his apartment, the better to start hiding a hundred bucks of liquor around his rooms where Drunk Wil can't immediately drink *all of it*.

The last bottle he holds onto, propped against the door of his offices with his phone in his hand. He stumbles around behind his desk and opens the window out of habit, ready for the cigarette smoke that there won't be, because he doesn't have ... any ... Kemp reaches into his pocket and finds a pack of twenty.

With a grunt of effort and a twinge in his upper arm, he turns to throw them out of the window–

"Checked your desk yet?" Dempsey murmurs pleasantly, and hangs up right after.

Kemp drops his phone as if it's poisonous and backs away from the window, still clutching the cigarettes tight enough to crush them. He drops into a crouch, trying to present as little of a silhouette against the glass as he can, and reaches up for the drawer handle.

There's about a fifty-fifty chance it's rigged to explode; Dempsey doesn't usually go in for big showy bombs, he's a very *hands-on* kind of guy (unwanted, Kemp's mind supplies a graphic reminder of exactly what that means), but he's also a pragmatic pervert and this will at least be easier than running him to ground if necessary...

The desk drawer does not explode in his face and kill him which is, Kemp thinks, a start.

Kemp pulls himself up level with the desk by his fingers and peers inside. There is only a sheet of paper torn from a notebook, and it doesn't appear to be hiding anything else. He exhales very slowly, drops the cigarettes on the floor, and scissors his fingers to grip the innocuous-looking note.

He opens the note, his thigh muscle jumping. It says, in the childish handwriting of a man who got into pimping via a route that didn't really include finishing high school, "*None of my boys have seen him lately but Crista says he did about two weeks ago. His number is—*" and a near-incomprehensible slew of digits. Sadly there is a little more to the note: "*You owe me.*"

"Is that meant to say Christian, you scribbly fuck?" Kemp asks the empty office, partly to stop his thigh muscle from twitching. It's probably not Dempsey who broke in and left the note, he's a busy man and will have just sent someone else, probably Henry or someone less in-the-middle-of-having-his-ass-eaten, but that doesn't help Kemp feel any less ... violated.

He laughs at the empty room and cracks open the bottle in his hand – vodka, cheap and nasty – before slumping down with his back against the window-wall and his feet against the desk, the note lying on his chair.

Fuck it all. He'll call Crista *tomorrow.* That's another day of fees from that ridiculously pretty idiot Carriere...

Kemp is vaguely aware of crawling under his desk and staggering back up the stairs to his apartment some time later, in search of the remainder of his stash, but of little else; his mind treats him to a full action replay of his kiss with Farinaux, the nearest he's come to sober action in *years.* Farinaux's tongue like an amorous octopus, his lips sucking the will out of him.

He realizes his hand is on his crotch, squeezing his half-hard dick through his trousers, at the same time that he realizes the mouth he's imagining is not Farinaux's unshaven maw but Carriere's luxurious lips and no doubt nicotine-tasting tongue.

"Fucking fuck no," Kemp slurs, clambering over whatever separates him from his bed – the contents of his closet, probably – and grabs the next bottle from down the back of his mattress. Drunk Wil needs to hurry the fuck up. He is not jerking off over his client sober.

He sags onto his back against the mattress, absently rubbing his groin with the back of his hand, arching his back as he swigs again. Drinking and jerking off at the same time *does* require a certain amount of coordination, but he's had a lot of practice.

He digs guiltily through his memory for images of Carriere's delicate, elegant hands and the place his neck becomes his shoulders, the surprising grace in his ungainly angles, his unbearably smooth and clear skin without a blemish or a hair. He looks like a statue carved by a pervert.

But Kemp's brain, still too sober to allow Drunk Wil's hand at the ... tiller ... although apparently drunk enough to knock his equilibrium for six, unhelpfully offers a play-by-play account of the night he first learned precisely how Dempsey felt about having his affairs meddled with; the sound of choking, the look of triumphant anger and *amusement* on Dempsey's face, the aftermath of a brutal murder–

Kemp swirls cheap gin - it seems to be gin - around his mouth but his mind is in no hurry to relinquish the path it's embarked on.

His hand, apparently independent of any desire in the rest of him, continues to grope and rub his cock through his pants, even as his brain pursues memories he'd rather not dwell on. Kemp's face feels hot and flushed, as if someone has slapped it, and the memory of being backed against a wall with a snarl, unpainted brick scraping his as yet untattooed skin, the memory nauseates rather than arouses him. But his hand doesn't stop.

Perhaps Drunk Wil has his hand and not his mind. Kemp screws his eyes shut and hopes that he won't remember this in the morning.

Dempsey has methods which, being a creature of habit, he probably hasn't changed; Kemp's lips draw back involuntarily, his mouth pressing open and his tongue flat against his jaw at the memory of leather belts, the "breaking in", and all the fragments which Drunk Wil is supposed to protect him from. "C'mon."

His hand has slid inside his pants now, clutching the base of his cock as it grows more uncomfortably tight in his pants, bent to the side and almost wholly hard.

He drags his mind back to Carriere guiltily; his guileless eyes with their light eyelashes, his silly cologne. The feel of his shirt on Kemp's face. In some other life where Carriere's not a moron letting Sickert spunk diseases into his body cavities, and Kemp's not an alcoholic who feels like a constant failure, hiding in the shadows of his rat's-nest apartment from the shadows cast by his own youth, they'd be a hot couple.

Kemp squeezes his cock and showers himself with the end of a fricative sound, caught between his teeth and his lower lip. There is a groan trapped somewhere in his chest, vying for release from his throat;

Carriere has a mouth made to suck men off. Carriere has, no doubt, pubes the color of a tequila sunrise. Carriere's dick probably tastes of *hope*.

Not before time, Drunk Wil steals into Kemp's head and almost gently relieves him of responsibility – or at least, this is the latest Kemp can remember when he wakes, retching and disoriented, his head dangling off the mattress some time just before dawn.

"Fzzzuck," Kemp grumbles, champing his jaw groggily a few times. It takes him a minute or so to get the ceiling into focus and for him to stop feeling like all the blood in his body has been stolen from him while he slept.

Further investigation reveals that Drunk Wil's agenda for him includes the instruction to *PHONE DVORAK*. This message is left both on the back of his hand in ballpoint, on the side of his shitty dorm refrigerator in what looks like ketchup and which he is not injured enough for it to be blood, and one final time in Sharpie on his bed sheets.

Drunk Wil is obviously keen for him to call this Dvorak. Kemp is baffled: Drunk Wil tends not to involve himself in detective work.

After a moment or so of wary prodding at his own memories, Kemp recalls that "call Dvorak" was part of his itinerary for the day anyhow, and though he takes the trouble to dress properly before stumbling down to his office he finds himself half-expecting – maybe even half-*hoping* – that Carriere will blunder in again.

However, there is no sign of the stringy French redhead, and Kemp's left to dial the scribbly number from his ominous note unmolested by dolorous eyes.

"Hello," says an accented, androgynous voice in a throaty and – if Kemp is any judge, which he thinks he very much is – hungover whisper. "Crista is speaking."

"Mr. Dvorak," Kemp says, sprawling over his desk in expectation of a long interrogation, groping for his non-existent cigarettes in his pockets and finding only an unexpected scotch miniature bottle, empty. "My name is Detective Kemp, Zeke Dempsey said you might be able to give me some information on–"

"He said I wanted to talk to you," Dvorak corrects. "And it's pronounced Dvorak."

Kemp takes a long, quiet breath and wonders despondently if Drunk Wil has fucked this slippery dickwad. He even *sounds* diseased.

"So, do you want to talk to me?" Kemp asks, instead. The opening salvo of the day's rain begins to batter the windowpanes behind him, even though it's barely even noon. "Or did I remember that wrong, too?"

"No need to be moody," Dvorak says, his accent rendering the sentence an interesting listen for Kemp's still-suffering ears. "Zeke said you're looking for Sickert."

"I'm being paid to look for Sickert," Kemp corrects, pettily.

"My apologies."

"So," Kemp says, rubbing his bicep with his free hand: it hurts, and he has no idea why, "do you have any idea where I might find him, where he might be?"

"He might be passed out across my thighs at the moment," Dvorak says slyly, "or he might not. What's it worth?"

Kemp sits bolt upright, but he doesn't let the change in position show in his voice. "How much do you *want* it to be worth?" he asks, keeping the epithet *whore* purely mental.

"Oh we can discuss that later," Dvorak says airily, his accent making it sound somewhat more threatening than if it had come out of Baron's mouth (though that would presuppose Baron didn't have something *in* his mouth at the time, Kemp thought, automatically scathing). "Would you like an address?"

"Of course," Kemp says patiently, rubbing his bicep again. It feels bruised. Drunk Wil's insistence on injuring him is weird.

"That will also cost." Dvorak has the voice of a man-boy who is winding his hair around his finger coyly. Kemp wants to slap him.

"I thought you said you would discuss that *later*?" Kemp points out. "And I can't come and give you your money if I don't know where you are. Or would you prefer I give it to Dempsey–"

Dvorak rattles off an address so quickly that Kemp almost doesn't catch it. He scribbles it down on his arm while it's still fresh in his memory and is confounded to discover shortly afterward that he is writing with an eyebrow pencil. The hell does all this stuff *come from*?

"Thank you, Mr. Dvorak," Kemp says, almost smiling into the phone. "How long do you think Sickert will be there for?"

"How long would you *like* him to be here for?" Dvorak all-but-leers.

"I don't know what Dempsey told you but I'm not *that* rich," Kemp sighs, standing. His shoes are unlaced. Oops.

"Oh that isn't a problem," Dvorak says peacefully, "*he* pays for that part."

"He's not ... dead?"

Dvorak laughs. "I am not a fucking retard, Detective Kemp, I don't kill the goose that lays the golden egg. He's staying here. If you want him so bad, come get him. With money."

Kemp nearly trips over his laces on his hasty way out of the office, and it's only when he nearly falls down the stairs as well that he puts a moment aside to tie them – in that moment he realizes he should probably – call Carriere, but it takes him a full handful of minutes, enough to see him out onto the sidewalk, before he can bring himself to do it.

"'Ave you called to say you are sorry for being so rude?" Carriere grumbles when Kemp finally presses the phone to the side of his face. The screen's already wet with the day's rain, his pants soaking up the drops that bounce back from the hot sidewalk.

"Yeah, sure, whatever," Kemp mutters, "I called to tell you I found your good for nothing boyfriend, you owe me another day's fees, and..." he coughs and looks at the sky, getting nothing but an eyeful of rainwater for his trouble.

"Where is he? Is he alright?" Carriere demands immediately, and Kemp can hear the sounds of scrambling. "Tell me where I can find him immediately, do you hear me–"

"...AND," Kemp repeats more loudly, "I need you to give me a ride so I can *get* to him."

"Why do you need to be there? I will give you your money later."

"Yeah, excuse me if I don't have an overwhelming degree of confidence in anyone's ability to actually make good on their fiscal promises," Kemp says, his sarcasm so strong that a woman walking her shitty little handbag dog flinches away from him. "I stopped *voting* ten years ago too, same reason. Nothing *personal.* Also I have a contact I need to pay off."

"Hmph," Carriere says, not very convincingly. "You won't tell me any more nonsense about how it is far too dangerous for me, then?"

"What would be the point? You won't listen." Kemp inspects his shoe as water begins to leak uncomfortably into his sock. "If you come get me from the Drake Liquor Store on the corner I'll give you directions from there."

"Thank you," Carriere says, surly and sullen and sounding deeply ungracious, "for finding my boyfriend."

"Thank me later and with money," Kemp says, hanging up. He's quite confident that

Carriere will not thank him in the slightest for bringing this to his attention, but at least there's the vague possibility that he'll have a little money left over from paying off Dvorak. Maybe enough to actually pay his fucking rent for once.

The specter of *you owe me* from Dempsey darkens his thoughts and Kemp tongues the roof of his mouth to distract from the possibilities *that* brings to bear on his mind.

The presence of an actual taste which isn't ashes and mucus still surprises him.

It takes Carriere a little longer to reach the liquor store on his stupid little *putt-putt* bike than it takes Kemp on foot, which leaves him wondering where, exactly, Carriere's own apartment is. It's probably somewhere *nice*, somewhere with a proper defense against roaches and mice that aren't the size of terriers, somewhere spiders do not treat the bathroom as their own, somewhere that has a super who isn't either dead or dying.

Today Carriere is wearing a leather bike jacket in spite of the clammy heat, open at the front to reveal a blue t-shirt on which a picture of Mickey Mouse with Dia De Los

Muertos make-up on has been painted in rhinestones and glitter-paint. He has on pants which appear to have been constructed from the anorexic corpses of other pants and an unfortunate bird. The motorcycle boots look distinctly out of place.

Kemp looks down at his damp Hush Puppies and tells himself to shut up.

"Where are we going?" Carriere asks, without greeting him.

"Money," Kemp says, holding his hand out. "Also, I should tell you you're not going to like what–"

"If he is *alive* and well I am satisfied," Carriere interrupts, with a heart-breaking expression – Kemp scrubs his brain carefully, quite certain he has nothing of a heart left to break anyhow – and he extracts another fat bundle of bills from his jacket as if he's never heard of narcotics patrols or looking suspicious, and presses the money into Kemp's hand abruptly.

He holds the back of Kemp's hand as he does, and his fingers are cold, his palm hot. Kemp jerks his hand away too fast, and shovels the bills into his pocket without checking them.

Kemp gives him the address and waits to see if Carriere will actually allow him to accompany him there; he is rewarded for his patience with a handful of motorbike helmet and a watery expression that he can't read very well.

Perhaps it's just the rain getting in his eyes.

The route to the address is a vexatious one; twice they have to stop to ask for directions, and on one of those occasions the newspaper vendor leers at them in a manner that suggests he thinks Kemp is Carriere's sugar daddy or some shit like that: Kemp thinks about how incredibly *wrong* that assumption is, but Carriere's back on the bike and pushing the pathetic little engine as hard as it will go before he can make up his mind which segment of the wrongness is most egregious.

The address turns out to be an unassuming apartment block built some time in the seventies and decorated by someone with no imagination and too many books about the Civil War; to Kemp's near amusement someone has painted an unconvincing trompe-l'oeil of a veranda on the side of the building out of what he can only assume was sheer cussedness.

The train has stopped, leaving ominous clouds and offensively claustrophobic air carrying so much warm moisture they might as well be trudging through a men's bathroom.

"Okay," Kemp says eventually, wishing he had a gun with him, as the super lets them into the building. "I'm just going to pay Dvorak and then I will get gone. Nice knowing you."

"Who?" Carriere asks without interest, stabbing the button for the elevator a few times, too hard and too fast.

"Dvorak," Kemp repeats, as if that is in any way helpful.

"*WHO*," Carriere snaps, glaring at him, but Kemp just slips into the elevator behind him and begins mentally calculating how much Dvorak can actually get away with asking him for.

"Eighth floor," Kemp says, pointing at the doors as they open.

"He is alright," Carriere says, stamping out of the elevator with more violence than someone that skinny should be capable of inflicting on the blameless floor.

"Yes, but I don't think–" Kemp says, hoping like hell that Sickert is either still passed out or getting ready to leave.

Kemp ducks around Carriere, narrowly avoiding contact with his jacket – it smells of cigarette smoke, car fumes, and some sort of cologne which has been engineered to smell of wood smoke and cathedrals which is unexpectedly attractive – and knocks sharply on the door to warn the inhabitants to get their shit together.

There is a shout of, "It's open," in an accent which Kemp recognizes as Dvorak's: he assumes the door has been opened in anticipation of their arrival and also that this bodes extremely badly for his own safety, never mind the deeply ill-advised trust in which Carriere seems to have spent a lifetime marinating.

"Maybe I should," Kemp begins, because he can at least *pretend* he has a gun on him, but he's already too late. Carriere shoulders the door open with a kind of burly impatience that sits ill with his fragile-looking frame, and steams along the narrow hallway like a furious housewife.

It occurs to Kemp that he possibly, maybe, recognizes Dvorak's voice too.

The explosion of French shouting reaches his ears before he makes it into the main room, and although Kemp's French is terrible at best he has an inkling of what he's going to see.

It doesn't render the tidiness of Dvorak's apartment any less unexpected, but it does at least mean that the sight of a naked-from-the-waist-down Sickert (Kemp very carefully focuses on a tattoo and refuses to be drawn into checking out the man's cock) and wholly-naked-but-for-make-up-and-an-iridescent-knee-sock Dvorak (he assumes it is Dvorak as school girls are not known for their testicles) slowly unraveling from whatever they were doing, still sticky, is no shock.

It probably wouldn't have been a shock anyway, Kemp thinks as Carriere – vibrant pink to the hairline and shouting incomprehensibly while Sickert smirks and Dvorak giggles – waves his arms and spatters the room with what is almost certainly invective.

He isn't a naive pretty idiot. One only has to look at Sickert to know he's a cheating lothario asshole, and Dvorak doesn't exactly give off an air of the wholesome.

"How much did you want?" Kemp says to Dvorak, because he *is* that stupid, and he thinks in that moment that the volume and volubility of Carriere's denunciations will drown out anything else or at least hold Sickert's attention… forgetting just how little Sickert plainly cares about the angry French boy.

"You trying to buy my whore off me?" Sickert asks, and his voice is something else, a real streak of oily self-indulgence. Of course he's British, or sounds it. What else would he be? He stares at Kemp with an amused smirk, stares at him from under drooping, disinterested eyelids.

Dvorak is also frowning at him. Kemp thinks it might be intimidating if he were not so very used to everyone in a room hating on him at once.

"Just pay him off for services already rendered," Kemp says with what passes for a smile under these circumstances. The atmosphere in the room is such that it only needs a tiny spark to ignite it, and somewhere in the back of his mind Drunk Wil is searching for matches.

"Hey, you lying fucking prick – I never saw you before in my life–"

Kemp draws his features into an expression that's more Drunk Wil's than his, and says, "Of course not, but oh what a pleasure it was to hear your tittle-tattling voice–"

"Fuck you," Dvorak snarls, sounding uncannily like a wronged Marlene Dietrich. He lurches to one side, back toward a pile of clothes dangling off the brown pleather sofa, and Kemp has a momentary idea that he's looking for something before there's an impossibly loud noise and an impossibly violent pain in his shoulder which spins him on his feet and leaves him face down on the champagne-colored carpet.

Ow, Kemp thinks in a detached manner, as he watches the carpet turn dark red beneath him. *That hurt.*

In the foggy white distance he can hear Carriere shouting, in English this time. Something about ambulances and the certainty of the police. Sickert's voice winds through the conversation like smoke through the damp streets, tainting everything with a poisonous calm, while Dvorak's slightly hysterical voice rises to clash with Carriere's, and the word *putain* is used a lot.

He knows he should keep a clear head, get up, and get out of the apartment and down to the ER before he either bleeds to death or gets a mercy shot in the head from Sickert, but Kemp feels instead giggly and elated, and his limbs are as much help as soggy string.

Kemp flops uselessly on his face, glued to the carpet by his own blood, and woozily considers how Carriere's voice is really quite musical when he's screaming in a frightened rage.

"Remind me to take you out to dinner," he says to the floor, trying to direct the words toward Carriere, as he passes out.

*   *   *

Kemp wakes to the smell of disinfectant.

"I can't afford this," he says as urgently as his mouth will let him, which means that what he actually says sounds a lot like *mmmrgglll tisstiss.*

At least nothing hurts. Everything feels wonderful. Amazing. Brilliant. Like morphine, in fact.

"You're awake," Carriere says, which Kemp feels is both unnecessary and a gross overstatement of the situation.

"Can't afford hospital," he repeats, clutching at the hospital sheets which appear to be tying him to the bed.

"Davey is paying for the hospital," Carriere says rather grimly. Kemp pries an eye open and peers at him through a cage of eyelashes; Carriere is wearing a plain white t-shirt and a slightly haggard look. He wonders if the boy has actually slept, and how long both of them have been here. "Because if he doesn't I have a lot of things I need to tell the police. And if anything happens to *me*, my mother will have a lot of information to give to the police instead."

Kemp is glad that his morphine-stupid mouth isn't up to making the surprised noise that sounds in his head. Clearly Carriere – Claude, he supposes – isn't as dumb as all that.

"And," Carriere says, with a certain finality and a twist of his impossibly pretty mouth, "my mother is in France. He cannot shoot *her*."

"I was going to ask you to dinner," Kemp mumbles before he can stop himself. The goddamn morphine clearly has its downsides, too – not least the way his head and feet currently feel as if they're residing in different states. His feet might as well be in Florida.

"You have a bullet hole in your deltoid," Carriere says.

There are flowers next to his bed. Kemp fervently hopes they're either from some charitable institution or from Carriere because if they're from anyone else he knows in this town they're not so much a Get Well Soon gift as a very blunt threat regarding the likelihood of him being stabbed in his sleep.

"When I don't have a bullet hole in my beltroid – deltoid – fuck these are strong drugs…"

"And how were you planning to pay for this meal?" Carriere sighs, folding his arms. Kemp finds keeping his eyes open is something of an uphill struggle, but for the sight of Carriere wearily and rather maturely interrogating his good intentions from the foot of his bed it's worth it.

The artificial light halos the boy's hair, like some Pre-Raphaelite saint.

"Sell my shoes," Kemp suggests indistinctly. He feels like his mouth has been packed with cotton balls and there's a persistent ache in his shoulder, which he thinks means the fucking morphine is wearing off before he can really face it doing so.

Carriere snorts. "No one would buy them."

Kemp feels a faint pressure on his feet and blinks in slow, stupid surprise. Carriere – Claude – is clutching his toes through the hospital blanket in a sort of reassuring gesture that Kemp flatly fails to remember anyone else doing.

"Maybe you should let me take you to dinner instead," Car–Claude suggests, patting him on the foot again.

"Do I have to wait until I don't have a hole in my shoulder?" Kemp asks, slightly giddy.

"At least until you can make words without sounding drunk," Claude says, giving him one final pat.

Long wait, Kemp thinks, falling asleep abruptly.

* * *

Kemp spends two more interminable days in the hospital eating tasteless cheeseburgers and watching horrifying daytime television. Sickert's money is paying for a private room and good drugs but he's bored out of his fucking mind. Claude visits him again on the second morning and at least has the decency to smuggle in good coffee for him even if he won't bring any liquor.

He blames the morphine for the way he whines when Claude gets up to leave. "Don't go, I'm going to fucking kill myself just to be not bored," he complains.

Claude just laughs at him. "I have to go work," he says. "The photographer is in from Berlin and can't reschedule so I can stay here and watch Oprah with you." He reaches into his backpack and tugs out a jumble of magazines and DVDs, dropping them on the table beside Kemp's bed. "I'm going to come back tomorrow when you get out, I promise. And then we will have dinner, alright?"

Kemp manfully resists the urge to pout at him. "Fine."

"Don't be a baby," Claude scolds him with a smile twisting his flawless mouth. The boy's smile is ridiculous. Kemp keeps judging himself for finding it *charming*.

"Can you adjust this godforsaken pillow before you go? Ratched out there hates me." The idea comes to Kemp in the moment between asking and Claude leaning over him. It's cheesy. It's ridiculous. It's probably something he saw in a bad movie when he was the kid's age.

It's perfect.

Claude smiles at him again and leans over the bed, over Kemp's face, and carefully fluffs the pillows behind his head. Kemp gets a face full of cigarette-scented t-shirt and a short burst of dull pain; the smell of smoke in his face is more distracting than the pain.

He reaches up with his good hand and catches the back of Claude's neck, pulling him down and mashing their mouths together, in what should theoretically be an awesome romantic cue-love-song kiss.

What really happens is Claude flails and is thrown off balance so he drops onto the bed hard enough to jostle Kemp's shoulder, and their mouths don't line up and Claude's nose is jammed against his uncomfortably. But the idea is there and it only takes Claude a second to get his balance back, and then Kemp is treated to an enthusiastic tobacco-and-coffee flavored kiss.

If Farinaux's tongue down his throat in Starbucks was undeniably sexual and lewd, and sleazy and dominating, Claude's mouth on his is sweet by comparison. Not that the kid tastes sweet, he tastes like an ashtray and the bottom of a coffee filter and it's like crack to his tastebuds, but Claude is kissing him like he has nowhere to be and nothing else he wants to do.

Kemp slides his hand around to cradle Claude's chin, feeling faint stubble under his fingers, and warm skin. This is much better than Farinaux's public tongue-raping.

Drunk Wil clamors in the back of his head. *Fuck him. Fuck his mouth.* He shoves that thought away: he wants to fuck Claude's mouth but he wants to remember it, god damn it, and Drunk Wil isn't allowed to have this one.

"MmmmKempihavetogo," Claude mumbles against his mouth, just when Kemp is starting to wonder if he can get a hand on the kid's ass without too much trouble. He registers the faint noise of a phone vibrating inside Claude's backpack. "That's my ride calling."

"Just another minute," Kemp says, running his thumb over Claude's lower lip.

"I can't," Claude says, kissing the corner of his mouth. He's gone too fast for Kemp to pull him back into a proper kiss. "I'll be back tomorrow. I'll pick you up when you're discharged. Don't kill any of the nurses."

* * *

Kemp is very glad to see that, when they reach the curb outside the hospital, Claude has not picked him up on the putt-putt motorcycle. There's a car driven by another impossibly pretty, lanky kid that Claude greets with a fist bump and a stupid grin. Kemp doesn't catch his name because it's about eighteen syllables long and sounds Dutch or something.

He is less glad that Claude apparently has a burgeoning criminal streak; the kid lifted his keys and went to his apartment to get him clothes while he was unconscious. He's not sure if it's Claude breaking in or Claude *seeing* where he lives that really makes him uncomfortable, though.

The ride back to Claude's apartment is awkward. Half of what Claude and the other kid say to each other is in French, the other half is in German or Portuguese or some other language Kemp doesn't speak, and anyways he keeps getting distracted by Claude's fingers curling around his own.

"See you Monday, eh Carriere?" The kid in the front seat says after he slams on the brakes outside a nondescript brick building. Kemp swallows the surge of profanity he wants to let loose when his shoulder hits the seat again. The angelic-looking kid in the front seat turns and leers at them. "Don't wear him out, Grampa, we have a shoot and I need him in good condition."

"Shut up, go away, I will pick you up at ten," Claude says, grinning and poking Kemp to get out. Kemp shuffles himself out of the car and nearly trips over the motorcycle he's been riding bitch on for a few days.

Claude bumps into him while he's catching his balance: Kemp doesn't bother with trying to look serious. He smiles at the kid and gets a short kiss in return. Kemp pokes back the vaguely familiar feelings in his gut when Claude takes him by the wrist.

"Come on, I'm on the fourth floor," Claude says, tugging him into blessed air conditioning and out of the swampy heat.

Claude's building isn't as nice as Sickert's but it's miles better than Kemp's own. Even the lobby has nice framed art and a comfortable looking doorman behind a desk. Kemp tries to look less like a sleazy sugar daddy but gives up when he realizes Claude probably dragged Sickert through this same lobby. He just avoids the doorman's gaze until they're in the elevator.

"So I thought you wouldn't mind if I just made dinner here," Claude says, leaning back against the wall next to him. The elevator is quiet, and new, and shiny: Kemp catches himself staring at Claude's reflection in the polished doors. "Since you still have a hole in your shoulder."

Kemp weighs the amount of energy it would take to deal with some underpaid bitter waitress and people against the likelihood that Claude's cooking is shit. He adds in the potential for getting Claude to go down on him and he's willing to take the risk of bad food.

He shrugs painfully and mumbles his agreement. It gets lost in the elevator's ding but the kid gets the gist.

Claude's apartment is cool and well lit, exposed brick and bright white walls. Kemp's first impression is that this is way nicer than any place he's ever lived, let alone when he was barely twenty. Claude chucks his backpack into a corner onto a pile of shoes that look like they cost more than Kemp's whole apartment. Kemp notices small piles of clutter in other corners, jackets and shoes and books. It's oddly reassuring.

"Um... make yourself at home," Claude says. "Do you want something to drink?"

Vodka, Drunk Wil insists. Sober Kemp reminds himself that it's not even five in the afternoon and he wants to actually remember fucking Claude. He resists asking for hard liquor and stares at the paintings on the wall. They look like really nice prints; he doesn't recognize them but they're a lot more tasteful than Sickert's giant nudes.

"Kemp?"

"Oh. Um. Just water," he mumbles. Claude disappears around a corner and Kemp follows him after a few seconds of standing awkwardly in the hallway. He finds himself in the kitchen. Everything is shiny steel covered in smudged fingerprints. "So do you cook a lot?" he asks, scratching at a crusted bit of something on the counter.

"Huh? I'm not going to poison you, if that is what you are asking." Claude finishes rustling around in a cupboard and turns with glasses. "Davey only kept me around so I could cook for him."

Kemp looks away from the kid's bitter frown. The window over the sink looks out into an airshaft. The person on the other side of the building is growing some sort of brightly colored plant in a window box; the only things anyone grows in Kemp's building are pot and fungi. He looks back when Claude pushes a glass at him. "No – uh – I just meant *do you cook a lot*," he mutters.

Claude's smile is still tight when he shrugs and he doesn't meet Kemp's eyes. "I do, I suppose," he says. Kemp looks down at the rim of his glass instead of watching Claude's face. It's easier than trying to deal with the way Claude reminds him of Dan, of how he used to be a decent person who knew how to comfort someone with that look of sad-angry-tired on their faces. Back before his automatic response to stress was *get drunk and come on someone's face.*

Drunk Wil thinks getting drunk and fucking Claude's face is a marvelous idea. Kemp regrets letting Drunk Wil have so much freedom in jerking off over the kid.

"So do you want pasta or something?" Claude asks after a few too many seconds of awkward silence.

"Yeah, or whatever," he agrees. Kemp is glad that the kid broke the quiet before he said something embarrassing. He briefly wonders if maybe kissing Claude again will make him stop wearing that expression. He's not as hard hearted as he likes to think he is sometimes, and Claude's forced blank-happy look isn't fooling him.

It fucking works in movies, and the last time he tried to pull a stupid cheesy move on Claude it worked, so he goes for it. Kemp puts his glass aside and closes the space between them, slides his arm around the boy's waist, and kisses him.

It's hardly anything at first. Kemp catches one corner of Claude's mouth, then the other, and then the kid doesn't exactly melt or swoon into his arms (Claude has too many angles and sharp bony points to melt or whatever it is chicks in movies do) but he gets skinny arms around his waist and that exquisite mouth kissing back.

Kemp has a momentary flash of *I could get used to this* when Claude's hair flops around his face and hipbones like daggers dig into his belly. *I used to be used to this.*

When he pulls back, Claude isn't grinning but he doesn't look sad any more, and there's pink spreading in his cheeks. Kemp pushes red hair off Claude's forehead and smiles back at him. He's having *feelings* again, which aren't related to wanting to get drunk. It's disconcerting to say the least, but Claude's fingers are still playing with the hem of his shirt and he can't be bothered to think about feelings while he's still having them.

"Go watch TV or something, I am going to make dinner," Claude says, and when Kemp apparently fails to move fast enough for him, the kid pinches his waist.

"Ow, ow ow fuck," Kemp whines, but he lets go. "Be nice to me, I'm still shot."

"If you are well enough to try to put the moves on me in the hospital you can handle a few pinches," Claude informs him, smiling again. "Get out of my way or you will get no food."

Kemp concedes defeat and leaves the kitchen, though he pauses at the door to leer at Claude's ass when he bends over to dig through a cabinet. He follows a trail of dropped and kicked aside clothing and stuff into the living room, where he's treated to a vastly different view than that of his own apartment.

Despite small piles of clutter in corners and spilling out from under a table, the place just looks cleaner than Kemp's apartment.

The lack of dead cockroaches and live spiders probably really helps with that impression, he thinks as he pokes around. There's a row of big windows near the ceiling, too high to look out easily but which let in floods of light. The sofa looks like an Ikea special but it's white and fluffy, so inviting and clean and wholesome-looking that Kemp sort of wants to shower before sitting on it.

He doesn't even *have* a sofa. He has a broken down recliner that doesn't recline and at one point had mice living inside one of the arms. And even that certainly doesn't face a TV the size of an oven, with game consoles stacked under it and DVDs piled to either side.

Kemp avoids the virginal sofa and goes over to a bookcase instead. Most of the titles are in French, though there are a few trashy airport paperbacks with titles like *The Tropic of DANGER* and *Murder Manual* and some really expensive looking cookbooks.

One shelf has a bunch of pictures: Claude with other scrawny boys in tight pants and stupid hair drinking what's probably liquor out of paper cups, Claude and another redhead in front of the Eiffel Tower making ridiculous faces, a middle aged woman with the kid's bright red hair in an expensive frame.

There's a frame tucked away behind the other ones, face down on the shelf. Kemp glances back towards the hallway – he can hear Claude mumbling to himself in the kitchen – and carefully picks it up. He's nosy, he can't help it. It's a good trait in a detective. The photo is unsurprisingly of Claude and Sickert, at some party or bar. Claude looks like he's trying very hard not to laugh, a hand on the tattooed asshole's knee and leaning in towards him; Sickert looks bored and irritated with whatever's happening around them.

Kemp looks closer at the background and sees an out of focus Dvorak sulking blurrily behind Claude's shoulder.

He puts it back as carefully as he picked it up.

Kemp pokes around the room a bit more, digging through the little bits of Claude's life that are lying around. There are movie tickets and empty cigarette boxes covering coffee stains on the table in front of the sofa – the kid likes mindless action blockbusters with lots of explosions, apparently – and a stack of smudged CDs under the table. Aside from having shit taste in drug dealer boyfriends and being unfairly pretty, Claude seems surprisingly *normal*.

When he runs out of things to look at, he meanders back to the kitchen. Claude is leaning over the stove and staring into a pot with his head cocked to one side; he looks like nothing so much as a large red heron assessing a fish.

"It smells good," Kemp offers up lamely by way of greeting. Claude looks at him and smiles through the cloud of steam rising from the pot.

"*Merci*. Since you're here, can you get me a – *passoire* – um… a strainer from that cabinet?" Kemp follows the line of Claude's pointing and fetches a colander from a jumble of pans.

Claude takes it and gives him a kiss on the cheek in return. Kemp pokes down the surge of warm *normal* feelings and Drunk Wil's immediate *kill it with fire give me booze* reaction to those sort of borderline-happy feelings.

"Can I help?" he asks. It seems like what he's supposed to say.

"You can sit there and compliment me some more and stay out of my way," Claude informs him, waving towards the tiny table in the corner. Kemp obeys and drops into a chair; he bites back the grunt of pain that makes him feel old and broken down.

Claude largely ignores him while he cooks, except for the smiles he tosses Kemp's way like crumbs to a bird. Kemp is impressed by how easily Claude does his thing, throwing things in a pot and making it smell like Kemp's died and gone to some French restaurant heaven.

"Get plates down, will you?" Claude asks after a while. Kemp is half-startled out of his contemplation of the boy's profile and whacks his elbow on the table. Claude turns at the noise and laughs at him. "Please try not to hurt yourself more, I do not want you to be too injured to do anything else tonight."

"Oh, shut up," Kemp grumbles, rubbing his elbow. At least it wasn't the arm with a bullet hole in it, he thinks as he finds where the plates have been hidden. Claude has a cupboard full of mismatched dishes, some chipped at the edges and others in horrible shades of Fiestaware.

He picks two less broken and less eye-searing plates out of the stack while Claude fusses with whatever's been in the oven; soon enough they're both crammed in at the tiny table with plates full of pasta and chicken.

"I can cut it for you if you need help," Claude teases, and Kemp makes a face at him. The table is small enough that their knees are touching under it – cheap furniture and city apartments aren't built for people over six feet tall – and it's awkwardly romantic despite the dull ache in his shoulder and chipped plate in front of him.

Kemp pokes at the chicken tentatively with his knife. The fact that Sickert was keeping Claude around for his cooking doesn't mean much. Fucker was British. He was probably happy eating slop.

Claude kicks him under the table. "You are going to hurt my feelings, Kemp," he says, and puts an exaggerated pout on his unfairly pretty face. Kemp kicks him back.

"Just deciding which part to eat first," he answers lamely, and cuts into the food. He's still hesitant at the first bite, but the first piece pretty much kills his hesitation. Claude can fucking *cook*. Kemp looks up and the kid looks pleased with himself.

"So it is not terrible, is it?"

"No, it's really good," Kemp mutters around a mouthful. It's an understatement. It's the best food he's had in a long damn time and Claude just threw it together the way he usually throws together liquor.

"It's nothing fancy." Claude's knee bumps against Kemp's again, then Kemp feels bony ankles hooking around his. The kid starts eating and Kemp feels like a creep for watching his mouth, his throat when he swallows. He's busted after a minute when Claude looks up and his cheeks are pink. "You are staring at me."

He mumbles something resembling an apology and Claude laughs. "I don't mind, but your dinner is getting cold."

Kemp drags his eyes off Claude's mouth and concentrates on eating obediently, not that it's such a challenge. He's genuinely sad when his fork hits the plate after a while.

Claude tugs the empty plate away from him with a smile and orders him out of the kitchen again. "Go go go go," he says, waving Kemp out the door as the plates clatter into the sink. Kemp shuffles down the hall and back into the living room. The sofa still looks irritatingly unsullied and he still can't bring himself to sit on it.

"It doesn't *bite*." Claude's accent does something vaguely pornographic to the word when the kid comes up behind him.

"You don't know that for sure," Kemp mumbles, even though he knows it's ridiculous. The couch is too wholesome to bite anyone.

"You are very silly." Claude's fingers hook through Kemp's belt loops and pull him away from the furniture; Kemp follows the front of his trousers towards a door he hadn't opened earlier. "I like it."

Claude opens the door into a dimly lit bedroom and drags Kemp inside. His eyes go straight to the bed. He half-expects another whore of a bed, but Claude's is at most a tease, nowhere near as slutty as Sickert's. It looks like the kid hasn't made it in a few days, going by the tangled sheets pushed to one side, but it's inviting.

"Are you going to stare at it all night or put it to good use?" Claude asks as he pulls his hands free of Kemp's pants. Kemp watches the kid bend down to untie his shoes and hesitates for a moment before doing the same. Claude's teasing is making his stomach do strange things, like he's in high school again and Peter is flirting with him.

He winces when his knees click as he stands, but Claude is waiting for him and he's barely got his balance before the kid kisses him.

Claude's fingers are cool against his jaw and his mouth is warm. Kemp finds the boy's waist with his hands, pulling him closer and ignoring the dull ache under his shirt when Claude's shoulder bumps his.

He could definitely get used to this, he realizes with an uncomfortable flop of his stomach. Not the burning in his shoulder from having a 35mm slug shot in and dug out, that part sucks. No, it's the part where Claude's fingers are curled around the back of his neck, or the way the kid sighs when Kemp kisses his neck.

"The bed is right there, Kemp," Claude says into his hair.

"You're the one that sidetracked me," Kemp points out. The bed is two steps to the left. He manages to keep his hands on Claude's hips when the boy steps back from him and peels off his t-shirt. Claude is white white *white*. If Kemp wasn't weirdly infatuated with the kid, he'd probably call him pasty, but he's not inclined to be a dick when he's about to *get* dick.

He drags his eyes away from the flat planes of Claude's chest – really, he's distracted by the kid's cotton candy pink nipples and resisting the urge to bite them is more work than he can really handle right this second – and tries to concentrate on making eye contact again. Claude, however, is busy with the buttons on Kemp's shirt and foils his attempts.

Kemp pulls him closer, trying to get their hips lined up, and bites at Claude's ear until he's shirtless, too.

He has to let go of Claude's hips to shake his shirt the rest of the way off his arms, but as soon as the cuffs are off his wrists he pushes the kid back towards the bed. It doesn't take much urging to get Claude onto his back.

It takes Kemp a little bit longer to get himself laid out on the bed next to him - he can't just fling himself down backwards right now and hope to land in any sort of elegant, inviting, *conscious* sprawl.

Claude doesn't seem to think he needs to be so careful. Kemp really needs to reevaluate his idea of this skinny kid as delicate or sweet because Claude is pushing him around like Kemp usually pushes skinny pretty boys around. He finds himself on his back with Claude's surprisingly substantial weight holding him in place and his perfect mouth pressed hard against his own.

Kemp's dick informs him that he had better not fuck this up. There is currently a very pretty boy with flawless lips and nipples that are just begging to be bitten and a throat made for swallowing his spunk lying on top of him.

It has been a fucking long time since he's gotten laid sober and he has absolutely no idea when he'd get another chance to fuck someone this hot.

His stomach is flopping around like a dying salmon and his hands might be grabbing at Claude's flat ass a little too hard but he's vaguely worried that Claude will decide he's not interested after all.

The room is quiet around them while they shift and squirm into something that works for both of them. Kemp loosens his grip on Claude when he's a little more certain that the kid isn't going to fuck off and kick him out before he gets to come at *least* once. Kemp likes the slow grind they settle into, hips rubbing together and wandering hands and easy kisses.

He ignores the insistent pulse in his balls where Claude's skinny thigh presses up against them; it's not until the boy slides sideways and replaces his leg with bony fingers that Kemp realizes Claude has a hard on trapped in his appallingly tight trousers.

Kemp follows Claude's lead gracelessly, fumbling at the front of his pants but getting distracted by the soft skin of his belly. Claude gets his elegant fingers into Kemp's pants before Kemp even manages to get the button undone.

The smug curl of Claude's mouth when he groans is irresistible and Kemp fails even harder at getting into the kid's pants because he can't keep track of what his fingers are doing *and* kiss Claude at the same time. Claude is better at multitasking than he is and undoes his own pants and kisses Kemp stupid, all while rubbing his dick with hot fingers.

Actually, it might be the hand on his dick that's making Kemp stupid.

Claude, the *asshole*, takes his hand off Kemp's junk well before Kemp is ready for him to, and shifts away from Kemp. He's about to follow after him, maybe climb on top of him and grind at that soft belly until he comes all over Claude's stomach, until he realizes that Claude is bending at unholy and gravity defying angles to get out of his fucktight pants.

That is a perfectly good reason for giving Claude a few seconds to himself. His pants are not nearly as difficult to get out of so he just watches Claude contort himself into nudity.

Claude's pubes are as flamingly red as the hair on his head. Kemp reaches over and drags his fingers through the curls, tugging just hard enough that Claude's hips jerk up after the pull. As soon as the kid kicks his pants off the bed Kemp gets a lapful of naked boy again.

"Why aren't you naked yet?" Claude demands with a grin and spots of pink on his cheeks.

"Because you're sitting on me," Kemp answers, running his hands up white thighs. All of Claude's body hair is the same bright pale red as his eyelashes. Kemp's fascinated.

"Oh, fine," the kid sighs dramatically and flops off to the side. Kemp pushes his pants down and struggles to untangle his feet from the legs; it takes more effort and concentration than he wants to admit in order to get out of his boxers.

When he's finally as naked as Claude, he expects to get his armful of redhead back, but the kid is sprawled across the bed away from him digging through a drawer. Kemp heaves himself over and drapes himself across Claude's back, very unsubtly grinding his dick against the pale curve of his ass and dragging his mouth across the boy's shoulder.

"You are very impatient, Mr. Kemp," Claude informs him, squirming around under him. Kemp grunts an agreement. He isn't about to admit how long it's been since he remembers fucking someone. He grunts again in *fucking pain* when Claude's squirming knocks his arm, and again when Claude pushes him over onto his back. "Oh – shit – Kemp?"

"I'm fine," he says manfully. "Gimme a second."

Claude's idea of *giving him a second* apparently means *distract him by sucking on his throat*. Kemp doesn't exactly mind, it's an effective method of keeping his mind off the dulling throb in his shoulder. Kemp's uninjured arm slides around Claude's waist, down to grope at the slight crease where pencil thigh meets flat ass, and the kid grinds down against him.

They both groan. Claude's mouth drags up Kemp's throat, until they're kissing again.

This time it's not sweet, or slow, or easy. It's eager and hot and dirty.

Claude's bedroom isn't so quiet any more. The shift of knees and hips and hands and arms makes the sheets rustle and the mattress creak softly. Claude makes quiet panting whines when Kemp squeezes his ass and pushes up against him. It's like nasty music to Kemp's ears when Claude's noises mingle with his own harsher grunts.

He's vaguely worried that he's going to just come from the humping like a fucking teenager until Claude pries one of his hands off his ass and shoves a lube packet into his hands.

"I do want you to fuck me," the kid mumbles against his mouth.

Kemp has to take a couple deep breaths at that to keep from embarrassing himself. He has a few false starts with the lube packet but finally gets it open, splattering some on Claude's sheets and dribbling down his palm.

He has slick fingers and it's a fucking start. A few seconds later his fingers are squirming into Claude's ass. The sound that gurgles out of Claude's throat is hot.

The way he shoves back onto Kemp's hand is fucking straight up pornographic.

Claude is a greedy bastard, grinding his dick into Kemp's hips and squirming back against his fingers and biting at his lower lip. Kemp digs his free hand into Claude's back and humps up against him. There's nothing even resembling a rhythm or any sort of grace to their movements. It's awkward and sweaty and sort of painful.

Every time Claude arches or bucks it jams Kemp's shoulder down and makes it ache again. His wrist is at a strange angle where he's fingering Claude's asshole. He's probably going to have bruises from Claude's stabby hip bones. And he's so fucking turned on he's still worried about coming as soon as he gets his dick inside the kid.

Kemp swears when Claude sits up. He pulls his hand free from the kid's ass and tries to sneakily wipe his fingers on the sheets. Claude makes a face at him – he's busted – but the boy's skin is all flushed and his mouth is sinfully red, so it's hard for Kemp to feel guilty.

Mostly he just wants to come, and soon, and either on or in Claude. Kemp runs his hand over Claude's dick, tugs on his pubes again, and Claude laughs breathily.

"Give me the lube," Claude orders, squirming on Kemp's lap. He waves vaguely towards Kemp's head and Kemp gropes for more slick. Claude takes it, opens it, and Kemp has to bite his lip when slippery fingers wrap around his cock. Deep fucking breaths. It's just fucking. Claude's hot but he's not that hot. He's just the hottest thing Kemp's ever had perched next to his balls, that's all. No pressure. It's only been like, two years, max, since he had sex sober.

Kemp has to close his eyes and bite his lip when Claude's weight shifts again, and then his dick is pressing up into the kid's ass. Claude moans above him and the sound goes straight to his balls. Kemp grabs at Claude's thighs. His hips shove up into Claude, hard.

"Fffou… fuck, Kemp," Claude whines. He arches and Kemp pushes up again. He's going to come, seriously. Claude starts rocking, small slow bounces on Kemp's dick. "Kemp?"

Kemp opens his eyes to get at least one good look at Claude before he comes way too soon and never gets to fuck the kid again. One good memory to fuck his hand to until he dies. And a good fucking memory it's going to be: Claude's pretty face, his mouth open, his hard cock and ginger pubes, all pink and sweaty and grinding on Kemp's dick.

He comes.

His balls are turned inside out and his dick is like a fucking volcano and he digs his fingers into Claude's thighs and he groans like someone's just punched him in the gut. His vision goes blurry around the edges and his heart stops and then explodes and starts back up with a kick. And Claude is still bouncing on his cock. Or at least he is, for another few seconds.

"Did you just *come*?" Claude asks, still making tiny greedy twitches with his hips.

"It's been a really fucking long time," Kemp mutters, not meeting the kid's eyes. He pets the red marks he left on Claude's legs.

"I am going to take it as a compliment," Claude informs him. Kemp groans again when the boy pulls himself off his dick and crawls forward, sprawling next to him on the bed. Kemp leans over and kisses his pouty mouth until Claude bites him. "But now you are going suck my dick because *some of us* have something called *stamina.*"

"It *is* a compliment," Kemp answers. He wants to be annoyed that Claude is making fun of him, but the kid is smiling his special-ed smile and it's sort of hard – ha, ha – to be irritated. He has a brief flash of being completely powerless against Claude's stupid smiles in the future.

He levers himself up and flops down the bed until he's face to balls with Claude's junk. There are bony fingers in his hair when he leans in and noses at the kid's flaming pubes.

He hasn't given head (that he remembers, there's no accounting for what Drunk Wil's done) since the last time he fucked someone sober. Kemp pets at Claude's legs absently. It's not that he's nervous, he just wants to sort of redeem himself. It's weird and it makes his stomach do its high school flip-flops again.

"Smelling my dick is not the same as sucking it, Kemp," Claude informs him, tugging on a chunk of his hair.

Kemp pulls on Claude's pubes again in retaliation, but he stops dawdling. He shifts his weight onto his non-injured arm and drags his tongue over the head of Claude's dick. The kid pushes up and Kemp takes the cue. He goes to work and goes down, trying to remember all the tricks he picked up turning tricks.

Apparently his memory is better than he thought, or Claude's just really enthusiastic, but the kid can't keep his hips still or his mouth shut. Kemp flatters himself a little and tells himself it's the former. He slides down until Claude's ginger pubes are tickling his nose again and gets a desperate moan out of the kid.

"Kemp… unh… *fuck*," Claude whines. Kemp looks up through his hair when Claude tugs again, choking a bit at the awkward angle of cock-in-mouth. The hand that's not occupied with pulling just a little too hard on Kemp's hair is groping at his own belly and from what Kemp can see, his mouth is hanging open to let out those fuckhot little moans. "*Fuck*."

That's all the warning he gets before Claude's hips are twitching up and there's a rush of French jizz into his mouth.

He swallows as best he can but he splutters. French come tastes exactly the same as all the American jizz he's had in his mouth. It does not, in fact, taste like hope or any sort of magical sexy cure-all. Kemp lets Claude's dick slide out of his mouth and wipes his lips to catch the very classy dribbles, then hauls himself up the mattress to flop next to the kid.

"What were you saying about *stamina?*" he mumbles, hoping Claude isn't one of those guys who doesn't like post-fuck snuggling. Kemp's not embarrassed that he likes getting a bit of a cuddle. It doesn't make him any less of a man, god damn it.

"Shut up," Claude says. Apparently he likes snuggling just fine because he rolls half on top of Kemp and kisses him lightly. When he pulls back he's laughing and picking at Kemp's face. "You have… you have pubes in your beard."

Kemp can't help laughing at that, too. Claude holds up the red curlies he's removed from Kemp's face triumphantly, then scatters them off to the side. Kemp hooks his arm around Claude's waist and kisses his smile. Claude laughs and yanks on Kemp's chest hair lightly, so he bites the kid's lip.

"Why where you with Sickert?" Kemp asks after the stupid giggling dies away and Claude's face is buried in his neck. The boy sighs and kisses his throat.

"That is a little personal for a first date," Claude informs him, but answers anyway, with the air of a man who has been thinking about this for a while. "He was nice to me, really. He was rich, and smart, and he was fun when he wasn't being a dick. I didn't... well I knew... I knew he wasn't exactly a good person. I just didn't want to know how much of a fuck he was."

Kemp presses his mouth to the top of Claude's head and inhales the smell of his hair. He smells like sweaty boy and smoke.

"But now he's fucking gone, and he's too busy trying to clean up this whole mess with Dvorak and he's got Dvorak's – his pimp – after him, and I am done with cheating asshole criminals." Claude pulls his nose out of Kemp's neck and props his chin on his sternum instead.

"I won't cheat on you with contagious Eurotrash," Kemp feels compelled to inform him.

"I think I'd rather hear 'I won't cheat on you with anyone,'" Claude says, smiling faintly. "But I suppose it's a start." Kemp pushes the red fringe off Claude's forehead and pets his cheek awkwardly. He's starting to have all these *feelings* again and they're messing with his ability to be a dick.

"I won't cheat on you with anyone. But you have to be nice to me," he says quickly, and immediately feels stupid.

"Of course I will be nice to you." Claude nods his pretty head and digs his chin further into Kemp's chest. "*Merde*. Do you mind if I smoke?"

Kemp shrugs. "It's your place." He'll just have to somehow grow a stronger will in the next few seconds if he doesn't want to beg for a drag.

Claude grins and climbs over him to dig through the same drawer as before. Kemp leers at the rather attractive view he gets, the kid's ass in the air with a nasty and incredibly appealing smear of Kemp's spunk on his skin. He runs his hand down the back of Claude's thigh.

There's a surge of something almost warm and fuzzy in his gut when Claude tumbles back down next to him, lighter and nearly empty pack of cigarettes in hand, and kisses him. Kemp wraps his arms around the kid's back and kisses him back thoroughly.

"Can I have a smoke break before we go again?" Claude asks when Kemp lets him go, bumping his perfect nose against Kemp's. His face is out of focus but Kemp thinks he's smiling.

"Yeah, if you let me have one," Kemp says, and kisses him again.

About the Authors

Melissa Snowdon is a British writer and craftsperson living in London.

Dionysia Hill is an American writer and art historian living in Illinois.

Neither of them should be trusted to write fiction and yet somehow this book exists. Both authors would like to thank Amy Macabre and Cindy Rosenthal for untangling their mutual grammatical incomprehensibility, and to apologize to the world at large for writing.

www.ingramcontent.com/pod-product-compliance
Lightning Source LLC
Chambersburg PA
CBHW072144280526
45788CB00002B/779